FANS
Not Customers

FANS
Not Customers

How to Create Growth Companies
in a No Growth World

VERNON W. HILL II

with **Bob Andelman**

Foreword by **Tom Peters**

SECOND EDITION

P

PROFILE BOOKS

First published in Great Britain in 2016 by
Profile Books Ltd
3 Holford Yard
Bevin Way
London WC1X 9HD
www.profilebooks.com

3 5 7 9 10 8 6 4 2

Typeset in Minion by MacGuru Ltd

Printed and bound in Great Britain by
Clays, St Ives plc

A CIP catalogue record for this book is available from the British Library.

ISBN 978 1 78125 756 2
eISBN 978 1 78123 313 0

FSC
www.fsc.org
MIX
Paper from
responsible sources
FSC® C018072

What People Are Saying About Vernon Hill

"I liked Vernon Hill immediately because he's such a positive character … I think there are some Americans who take to England, particularly London, like a duck to water, and some that don't. Vernon and Shirley love London. They love meeting all sorts of interesting people, and that comes across. People here like Americans very much who like our country. Metro Bank is a *classic* mom and pop business. I think Shirley Hill does a fantastic job in building the Metro stores and brand. I'm very fond of Shirley because she's a hell of a character, and she's very warm. And I get on with her like a house on fire."

Lord Howard Flight, member, House of Lords

"Vernon told me that the whole point of the company is that it's a symphony. The performance works because everything works in concert and so, if you don't buy it in its entirety, you can't ever get it to work for you. Vernon's competition over the years simply refused to learn from Commerce Bank."

William C. Taylor, author, *Mavericks At Work*

"I had the opportunity to sit down with Vernon Hill and pick his brains on starting a business. He gave me a copy of his book, *FANS Not Customers*. 'Read this book,' he said, and I did. A whole bunch of things we do at Second Home, my company, are taken straight from the book."

Rohan Silva, co-founder, Second Home

"In banking, there is certainly an over-emphasis on not failing. Don't do something different if you might fail at it. Vernon has not been afraid. One of the most important elements of his success is that he has not been afraid to try things that either nobody else does or that conventional wisdom says is wrong ... Vernon reinvented American retail banking. His focus on service created a true growth retailer. No one else has grown an American bank internally at 23 percent per year for 30-plus years. No one."

Tom Brown, founder, Bankstocks.com

"Vernon Hill gave me some of his time. He looked at my business model, told me what I needed to do, told me why this would work or wouldn't work in the financial world. He told me how to raise money and what the disadvantages would be. Using that knowledge, I went off and started one of the few private equity backed law firms in the UK."

Colum Smith, CEO, McMillan Williams Solicitors

To our loyal colleagues, investors, and customers.

To my partners, John Silvestri, Steve Lewis, Chris and Natasha Ashton, Gary Nalbandian, and Craig Donaldson for their dedication, loyalty and support.

And to my beloved wife and life partner Shirley, with whom I have shared an incredibly rewarding life's journey, memorable travels, vision of the future and success at work and at home.

Contents

Foreword

Tom Peters

Writing this foreword is easy—and impossible. The "easy option": Just include every page of the book in my bit here. That is, I didn't find *anything* not worth reading, in fact ingesting, nary a "non-Wow" in sight. Writing a foreword to this book is impossible: there is so much I want to say and say in detail—and commend.

No kidding, this is the toughest foreword I've done, because I won't know where to stop, and want to say so much more than space permits. Such as:

- The story of Commerce Bank and now Metro Bank is virtually one of a kind—they do so damn much right.
- The bank works, absurdly well, from a P&L standpoint. Hence, Doing the right stuff = Doing the profitable stuff.
- You can make money, lots of it, off a "customer service model"—there are skeptics galore. ("Fools," I call them. Sorry.) (Of course there is a problem, and a big one: You can lose your shirt with a "SORT OF good service" approach—which costs a ton and is not memorable.)
- The bank takes on the regnant business model—and clobbers it. They want me in the branch (and WHAT A

BRANCH!—more later) dealing with their folks face-to-face, not out of sight at the ATM or on the web.

- "Cost cutting is a death spiral"—that sweet music is worth the price of admission all by itself, to me—it's long been my religion. Commerce and Metro tell us there are two choices for "doing business": (1) cost-cut your way to prosperity; or (2) spend your way to prosperity. And the answer is: There is indeed an ALMOST SUREFIRE answer: spend!

- Spend. *Over*-invest in people. Over-invest in facilities. What could be more obvious? (And so rarely practiced by even our so-called "best" organizations—especially in banking.)

- These guys want—desperately almost—to shower me with attention. (Darn close to "love and affection"—yes, a b-a-n-k.)

- And the "me" is everyone! Forget the "high net worth customer." Forget the "80–20 rule": Metro wants us all!

- They want to make "AMAZE," "AMAZE-ing," "AMAZE-ness" as normal as breathing—and they're happy to use that "hot" word.

- These "bankers" not only want me—but they want my dog!

- They want me darn near "24/7"—the "7" for sure and close to the 24.

- They are—yes, a "bank"—colorful. They pig out on Red and BlueRed and Blue. Red and blue. And then more … red and blue.

- I'm a "design nut"—I think design matters, a lot and everywhere—JUST LOOK AT APPLE. "Cool design" in a "bank"—yup, top marks on that one too. (The word "matchless" comes to mind.)

- Back to the "business model"—they are foursquare

champions of Organic Growth. (I consider myself Public
Enemy Number One of the "marriage of dinosaurs,"
otherwise known as 90 PERCENT of mega-mergers.)
(Small, perfectly targeted acquisitions are okay; they don't
screw up the culture. Yikes, I've been preaching this to
deaf ears for 25 years.)

- Back to the business model redux: these guys believe that
  people will pay a little more (or accept a slightly smaller
  return) in recompense for knock-your-socks-off-all-the-
  time service.

- Commerce believed they could "make it in Manhattan"—
  and did they ever; "instant success" was just that.

- Commerce "proved it," not only with profit but also with
  tiptop awards from the likes of J.D. Power. (And some
  amazing testimonials from tough cookies, scattered
  throughout the book.)

- They believe you can go for fast growth—and keep the
  spirit intact.

- They hate-hate-hate bureaucracy. So do I!

- They love training—call it what it is, "indoctrination" or
  "boot camp" for the company "culture."

- They groove on the word "Yes" (to customer requests) and
  treat "No" as if it were a four-letter word, not a mere two.
  Yes = Of course we can, just watch us. "No" = Mortal sin,
  not in our vocabulary.

- Customer service at this level costs money (learn inside
  about the expensive change machines, not to mention the
  cost of dog biscuits and balloons); and Metro spends that
  money.

- If you're going to give great service to your customers, then
  you've got to put employees "MORE first"—the "Thanks for
  the good work" parties are concocted with the brakes off.

- "*Kaizen*" is fine—do stuff a little better. But the Commerce and Metro story is not about "a little better"—it's about in-your-face-over-the-top-visible-all-the-time better.

Believe it or not, these 24 bullet points amount to no more than scratching the surface of the surface, offering you the tiniest of hors d'oeuvres. As I said, only going "ditto" to the whole book would do the whole book justice.

This is a bit weird. Why in the hell would Metro Bank give away its secrets in such startling detail? Well, it's fun to tell a great tale. But I'll tell you something else—this book is darn near un-copyable. (The authors may balk at that—tough.) Why? Because it requires a level of sustaining commitment that is stratospheric. No doubt one can pick up "a tip or two"—it won't hurt and it will probably help. But to be able to support such a contrarian model in the face of Monster Competitors means aiming for and delivering on over and over and over what my marketing guru pal, Doug Hall, calls "Dramatic Difference." What Vernon Hill calls "AMAZE"—day in and day out (remember, damn near 24/7).

I'd add one or two more things. The book works for a woman starting a one-person accountancy. Or for a CEO of BigCo trying to stand out in a crowded market. It does not work for the faint of heart—to be this different takes guts, and takes equal devotion to "the vision thing" *and* "the execution thing"!

There is a Hall of Fame, or at least my Hall of Fame, of the Customer Service Kings. It includes the likes of Starbucks, Whole Foods Market, Four Seasons hotels, Cirque du Soleil, London Drug in western and central Canada. And Gary Drug on Charles Street in Boston—a block from my home. And, the equal of any: Vernon Hill's Commerce Bank and Metro Bank.

Way to go Commerce—and Metro!

To readers:

- Enjoy!

- Learn!
- Steal!
- Implement!

And think seriously, very very seriously, if you are ready to commit to and to create and to adhere to a "culture" that supports this "absurd" level of service. I'D NEVER MAKE A "GUARANTEE"—LIFE IS TOO COMPLEX FOR THAT. BUT I WOULD BET A PRETTY PENNY THAT MANY A PRETTY PENNY WILL BE YOURS IF YOU FOLLOW SOME CLOSE KIN TO THIS APPROACH.

Tom Peters,
author or co-author of many international
bestsellers on business and management,
most notably In Search of Excellence, *which*
one survey rated the "greatest business book of all time."

Welcome!

Despite appearances to the contrary, this is not a story about building banks.

Really, it's not.

Does your bank open earlier than any other, close later than the competition and welcome you every day of the week?

Does it let one person tell you yes, but require at least two to say no?

Does it invite your dog inside for a treat?

Does it educate and entertain your children?

Does it produce FANS, not customers?

That sounds like only one bank I can think of: Metro Bank, which I founded in London in 2010.

Again: this is *not* a book about building banks.

Metro Bank sees its banking business as a retail operation more akin to Apple than the Bank of England; we open stores, not branches. We recruit colleagues, not employees. We distribute, free of charges, millions of promotional pens. Use them on the premises, take them with you and share a Metro Bank pen with your friends.

Our *raison d'être* is simple: we want *FANS*, not customers.

FANS Not Customers shares lessons from my experiences

with Commerce Bank in the United States and Metro Bank in the United Kingdom. These are hard realities that I hope will help you in reconsidering your own business in the days and years to come.

Don't read *FANS Not Customers* in the same way you would the tale of a traditional bank. We go head-to-head with them, but we're not one of them. We represent a retail experience you won't soon forget—and we think *your* business should, too.

This is a book about exploiting your potential as a company or an employee. Whatever describes you, I hope that you'll find ideas and methods in the pages that follow that will make you a greater, more valuable asset to yourself and your company.

To my fellow entrepreneurs:

- recognize and grasp your opportunities as they present themselves;
- learn how you can deliver value, differentiation, and improvement;
- believe in the importance of branding;
- understand that hope is not a plan;
- grasp that no one needs a "Me, Too" anything;
- proceed knowing that value creators are wealth creators.

Metro Bank is definitely not your mother's experience of a bank.

And this is definitely not a story about the banking industry. Be all you can be!

Vernon Hill
London
May 2016

Introduction: Start-Ups, Upstarts and Disruptors

The best way to predict the future is to invent it.

Alan Kay, co-creator of laptop computing and graphic user
interfaces, and the man whose work directly influenced the
creation of Apple's Macintosh computer

Great customer-focused retail brands are few and far between:

- Apple
- Four Seasons Hotels and Resorts
- John Lewis
- IKEA
- Amazon
- Harrods
- Commerce Bank and Petplan in the US, and now Metro
  Bank in London

My life's focus has been on creating great brands and great
companies. In this book, I share my philosophy of business and
wealth creation. You'll learn how to build companies that have
value to customers, investors and yourself. And if you're a team
member of one of our own businesses, including Metro Bank

and Petplan, you'll learn exactly what is expected of you and how to chart a path of growth, accomplishment and success.

With me, every conversation about building a great brand, generating wealth and creating fans, starts with three primary elements:

Differentiated *Model* +
Pervasive *Culture* +
Fanatical *Execution* =
FANS not customers

It's a customer service-centric business model that I believe can be applied to any business, in any industry.

Steve Jobs, co-founder of Apple, believed in the highest possible levels of customer service but not necessarily in giving the customer what he thinks he wants. He told biographer Walter Isaacson, author of the 2011 bestseller *Steve Jobs:*

Some people say, "Give the customers what they want." But that's not my approach. Our job is to figure out what they're going to want before they do. I think Henry Ford once said, "If I'd asked customers what they wanted, they would have told me, 'A faster horse.'" People don't know what they want until you show it to them. That's why I never rely on market research. Our task is to read things that are not yet on the page.

Jobs ignored market research and never ordered it. And I never have, either. He had an innate ability to see beyond what market research could tell us. If you're inventing the future, what is market research going to tell you?

Successful entrepreneurs have an informed instinct that guides their decisions.

*

I founded Commerce Bank in southern New Jersey in 1973. When we took the concept into Manhattan 28 years later, the financial press saw red. How could a little bank from New Jersey compete in the Big Apple? Reporters and columnists that failed to do their homework didn't realize that we had already established and proven a unique customer model, and exactly the same thing happened when we introduced Metro Bank to London in 2010.

How could this no-name, no-brand new bank compete with the British high street banks? All the market research said it couldn't. It said the British wouldn't switch banks under any circumstances. But we were about to deliver something that market research couldn't measure, a level of service that people couldn't compare with anything they previously experienced: a unique retail experience. We arrived and gave people the unexpected: real service and convenience.

In May 2000, Apple's value was one-twentieth of Microsoft's. In August 2012, Apple became the most valuable company in history. The iPhone and the iPad were not lucky flukes. They were the natural result of the progression Jobs spent his life perfecting.

No matter how much a company brags about itself, customers know the truth. They may buy a Windows PC or an Android mobile phone because that's what their company requires, but they're nowhere near as happy as the Apple user who is literally a fan. John Lewis and Harrods in Britain, IKEA, Carrefour, Four Seasons, and Starbucks, worldwide, similarly prosper by redefining customer service.

How do I know that Commerce Bank (and now Metro Bank) created *FANS not customers*? I could say it was the intense loyalty that developed around the brand. Or I could let Tom Petro, senior vice president of J.D. Power and Associates, a leading customer service research firm, do the talking for me:

Commerce applied out-of-the-box thinking to what is

normally a fairly buttoned-up business. What Commerce has done so well is to figure out what their niche is. With Commerce, it's about friendly service and convenience, kind of the everyman's bank ... According to the voice of the customer that J.D. Power is hearing, Commerce just does a great, great job and stands out among the crowd.

Fans tell their friends about you. They join your team. At family and friends' barbecues, they tell everyone about something magnificent your employees did for them, above and beyond the call of duty. They don't patronize you, they *become* you.

The premise of this book is to demonstrate how Metro Bank and Petplan employees build fantastic value by creating fans. It's the *Good to Great* story with real-life examples from someone who lived them.

Great businesses attract new customers, retain these customers and watch as happy customers become fans and recommend their family and friends: *FANS not customers*!

*

This is the second edition of *FANS Not Customers* and, since the original printing, Metro Bank has enjoyed tremendous success, received media attention around the world, and been recognized with numerous awards for everything from outstanding consumer service to cutting-edge technology.

I wrote this book as a guide to help you build your own business rather than just to tell the Metro Bank or Petplan story. These companies are used as examples of the themes, but the idea is to give you the tools to configure your own enterprise for maximum success.

When I give a speech, I encourage business leaders in the audience to steal these ideas and apply them in building their own disruptive enterprises. As you'll read in the stories of UK lawyer Colum Smith (page 48) and government official-turned-entrepreneur Rohan Silva (page 163), that's exactly what more and more people are doing.

*

One more thing about this book and our businesses in general: I didn't do any of this alone.

In 1973, besides opening the doors at Commerce Bank, I married my wife, Shirley, on December 22. A graduate of the Pratt Institute in Brooklyn, she subsequently founded her own architecture and design firm, InterArch, and established a unique ability to unite architecture, design, and brand. With Shirley by my side, design is a major competitive weapon—one every entrepreneur should pursue.

Over the years, Shirley and I have been partners in creating the design and executing the unique brands and facilities of Metro Bank and Commerce Bank. She and her team created and executed the look and brand at Commerce, and she is a critical element in the look and the feel of Metro Bank. *She is the brand queen.*

Shirley's role is to interpret, preserve and enhance the brands as well as create a unique exterior architecture and interior design, as it was at Commerce and is now at Metro. I developed the business model and set the standards for Commerce Bank: "America's Most Convenient Bank." When I said things such as "the world doesn't need another 'Me, Too' anything," Shirley and the staff of InterArch, her architectural design firm, took a commoditized business and turned it into a retail brand. They added emotion, buzz, and fun.

One of the greatest examples of her work can be found in Metro Bank's Magic Money Machines, the free to use coin counting devices in every Metro Bank lobby. Imagine the moment the manufacturer rolled the prototype black boxes—measuring 36 × 24 × 24 inches, which, unvarnished, look like small refrigerators—into her office. Her job? Make them "AMAZE!" customers—and they became Magic Money Machines.

Making our companies soar is also about the development of environments, the attention to detail, and great respect for the creative aspects. Shirley gives our facilities the energy and positive vibe that customers love. She knows me and Metro Bank better than anyone else could after four decades on the job together; with her professional skills, who could I possibly trust more to get it right?

I believe that great design is a pillar of great companies, and when you go in our stores, you will be AMAZEd, too.

We've also discovered a new partner in London in the person of Metro Bank's CEO, Craig Donaldson. You'll learn more about him later; he is a person who lives and breathes the Metro Bank culture. Making the model and brand grow in the UK is a personal quest for him because this is his country and Metro Bank is his bank. It's the application of our business tenets, for which he has spent his entire career searching.

*

These are the essential lessons that I hope you will take away from this book:

- No one needs a "Me, Too" anything.
- The brand is who you are, what you are, and what your customers expect!
- Hope is not a plan.
- Differentiate. Improve. Strive.
- You can try to cost-cut your way to survival, or you can grow your way to prosperity.

- Design is a competitive weapon.
- Value creators are wealth creators.
- Shareholders are your boss, your fellow colleagues—YOU!
- Stock options make every team member an *owner*.
- Ordinary companies are great at counting the parts, but do not understand the value of the whole. Companies with fans value the whole experience.

*

In these pages, I shall describe and expand upon our beliefs and experiences. I believe you have unlimited potential to be all you can be. Your company—large or small—needs you to succeed and grow. You have the potential to be a star.

To entrepreneurs, the future is yours. Each of you has unique talents, and if you are lucky enough to match these talents with your vocation, your future is also unlimited.

No one needs a "Me, Too" business or a "Me, Too" team member. You and your business need to add value, everywhere, every day.

Good luck in creating your own *FANS NOT CUSTOMERS*!

Part 1

Two Banks, Two Continents: A World of Lessons

1

Metro: The Revolution Comes to Britain

Dream more than others think practical. Expect more than others think possible. Care more than others think wise.

Howard Schultz, founder, Starbucks

As I stood on the steps of the London Stock Exchange, moments away from ringing the bell to make Metro Bank officially a publicly held company in the United Kingdom, I couldn't help but smile as my thoughts went back through the years leading up to this great moment in my life.

My banking career began with Commerce Bank, which I founded in New Jersey way back in 1973 and grew to $50 billion in assets and 440 locations—including Two Wall Street in Manhattan—before leaving in 2007.

Just three years later—July 2010—my wife Shirley, Sir Duffield, and I crossed the Atlantic and opened the doors of the first new British high street bank in 100-plus years, beginning five consecutive years in which our average compounded annual rate in deposits per store has exceeded 100 percent a year.

We crushed our original projections, growing at unimagined rates!

And now I was minutes away from seeing the London bank

I founded from scratch with a £20 million personal investment valued at £1.6 billion ($2.4 billion).

It was a dream come true.

Metro Bank exceeded our expectations.

As for the critics—of which there were many—they said an American-style, customer-centric bank selling service over rate wouldn't work in tradition-bound Britain.

But Metro Bank is a magnificent success.

We turned to the public markets on that day in early 2016 because we needed to raise more capital to support Metro's unprecedented growth and the time was right. I promised the original Metro investors that we'd go public in about five years. In Britain particularly, the markets saw it as a coming of age, a validation, recognition of Metro's success.

Metro Bank employs the bank model and culture that I developed in America and that was an unparalleled success for more than three decades. We exported it to the UK and plan for 110 offices in Greater London by 2020 and at least 5,000 colleagues and £25 billion in deposits. We Apple-ized the banking world in Britain, particularly in Greater London.

With one enormously successful grand opening in Holborn, Metro Bank changed the course of London banking forever. The revolution was under way.

*

Not that it was always easy.

There was, honestly, a culture clash in the beginning between our American model and the British public.

"This is nuts," the Brits told me. "This model of yours will never work here."

The *Times* asked, "Does this man know what he's doing?"

Banks in Europe were founded hundreds of years ago to finance the borrowing needs of governments. American banks were founded to serve the banking needs of local businesses and residents. Two fundamentally different systems!

Everybody wondered: could we break into the establishment? Metro Bank is a disruption model, an attack model. And we certainly attacked the establishment head on. Generally, people loved it. The establishment didn't expect it, didn't like it, or didn't care. But customers—potential customers—they love it. They all know their banks are bad. They all know their customer service is terrible—not unlike what we encountered when we broke into Manhattan in September 2001.

London is an even more international city than New York. There are a few differences that you won't find in New York City's melting pot culture, but the culture is much the same.

The British business culture frowns on asking for the sale. As a result, we have to train our colleagues that it's not rude to ask for the sale and that they must be more aggressive.

A man stood up during the question and answer session following a talk I gave in London and said: "Mr Hill, we Brits aren't very good at delivering service. How are you going to train us to do it right?"

"Are you telling me you're too stupid to be trained?" I asked, guessing he and the audience might be insulted.

And, in front of 150 people, the man said: "Yeah, that's what I'm saying to you."

Of course he was wrong. With our model, we attract and manage people who believe in building fans. It was hard to hire the right people with the right attitude in the beginning. But now that our model has been demonstrated and proven, day-in and day-out, for more than five years, it's easy to recruit, especially with the cartel banks dismissing thousands of experienced employees every year.

We came in with our American ways, which some here called "brash." But we just go out and hustle to earn business. The customers love it; they're just not used to seeing it. But this is no different from McDonald's or Starbucks coming to the UK, Europe and Asia—and they all succeeded.

*

It's been proved: Metro Bank works in London, even better than Commerce Bank ever did in New York.

Americans moving here, when they ask me what it's like, I say: "The people are magnificent, intelligent, personable and bear a sense of humor that takes some getting used to. London itself is absolutely stunning, from the River Thames vistas to the ancient architecture found at Parliament and modern designs such as The Shard. Be careful in traffic, though; it's every man, woman and child for themselves."

But let me tell you our story from the beginning.

*

Several weeks after my departure from Commerce Bank in the US, a London friend invited me to help him break through the century-old resistance of Britain's financial environment and build the country's first newly authorized retail bank since 1840. The experience has been nothing short of exhilarating.

We were the challenger bank with a disruptor business model ready to attack.

We created FANS by surprising and delighting every customer by:

- thinking like retailers while being the most professional bankers;
- exceeding customer expectations every day;
- working as one team—every customer matters;
- building the bank one store at a time.

5 March 2010, London
FSA banking license granted to Metro Bank plc

29 July 2010, Holborn, London
Metro Bank plc opens for business

7 March 2016, London
Initial public offering (IPO) values
Metro Bank at £1.6 billion

1 May 2016
700,000+ customers served by 2,000+
colleagues across 41 stores

We have to be AMAZE(ING) every second of every day.

We offer banking focused on the customer through unparalleled levels of service and convenience. With our unique, customer-focused business we reinvent the rules of retail banking, making every effort to remove all stupid bank rules from our services to offer simpler and more convenient banking to our fans. Our stores (a term we prefer to "bank branches" because there is nothing traditional about our sites) are open seven days a week, which demonstrates our commitment to customers that we're open for *their* convenience, not ours. And our call centers—we call them AMAZE Direct—never close, with live colleagues answering customer questions and solving problems 24/7/365.

Our iconic Metro Bank stores are just one part of our unified delivery channels. From mobile banking and online banking, and from 24/7 call centers to seven-day in-store banking, we deliver the best of every channel.

Metro Bank is an absolute growth business, from the model to the culture and beyond. It comes to us in two ways: the growth of comparable store deposits within our current stores, and opening new stores.

Comparable store growth is at the core of any retail organization's desire to be great. Existing stores must grow and new ones must open—or companies die. Time and time again, year-on-year store growth is the only way to know if a new store will succeed.

Great entrepreneurs shape the world around them, instead of letting the world shape them. And successful entrepreneurs succeed on informed instinct.

As a power retailer, Metro Bank delivers a best-in-class, value-added experience to everyone it serves, including individuals, private banking customers, and governments.

In our world, Metro Bank is nothing like a bank at all. It has "bank" in its name, but that's about it.

In all our stores you'll encounter face-to-face service with no requirement to book an appointment to discuss your banking needs. We instantly open your new personal and/or business account—often in 15 minutes—and offer card and cheque printers on site so you can walk away with everything you need to start using your account immediately. Call us on the phone and you'll receive unparalleled service from a live person, 24 hours a day, 7 days a week, 365 days a year. We aim to exceed the expectations of our customers every day.

The day we opened the first Metro Bank store in London, July 2010, the place was a complete mob scene, not unlike the arrival of the first Apple Store in Beijing in 2012. The excitement was broadcast live on BBC One for three hours—that's right, people in the act of opening new current and savings accounts captivated an entire nation. It was a scene of extraordinary excitement.

*

Did the world need another bank? When we came to London, we knew immediately that what this great city didn't need was one more "Me, Too" bank. Nobody buys an iPhone because it's the cheapest. They're buying the Apple experience. What the UK needed badly in banking was something it lacked: outstanding customer service and convenience.

As construction proceeded apace, we were told by "the experts" that our colors were too bright and we were far too brash, that "Love Your Bank At Last" was far too in-your-face, that our "Dogs Rule" campaign would never work, and as for "Kids Rock," well, we shouldn't say "rock" about kids. We were told by experts, "You should use pastels, maybe a light green and a soft yellow."

We dismissed all this misbegotten advice. Something that propelled our confidence was the early hiring of Craig Donaldson, our CEO. He is responsible for providing executive leadership to the bank's team. He is charged with guiding the bank's evolution from fresh, new entrant in retail banking to trusted financial services partner to millions of British customers.

From helping define Metro Bank's brand values, to hiring its inaugural employees and ensuring that the bank's staff deliver daily customer delight, Craig has been instrumental to Metro Bank from day one. His previous roles included managing director of retail products at RBS, as well as senior roles with Barclays and HBOS.

But despite his credentials, Craig is as unlike a typical British banker as anyone I've ever met. He spent most of his career railing against the stuffy London high street habits of inconvenient bank hours, lousy customer service and countless stupid rules.

Furthermore, Craig studied the Commerce Bank model at Harvard Business School in Boston and experienced it in action in the mid-2000s. He knew the British banking business could be better than it was, and after seeing Commerce create *FANS not customers*, he grew even more frustrated with business as usual back at home.

"I was probably seen as the guy who always railed against it from the inside," Craig told me. "I always knew this could work. What's not to like about service and convenience? But it could only be created from scratch."

When we brought Metro Bank to the UK, Craig was a natural to lead the revolution.

*

Many media reports on the grand opening of the first Metro Bank at Holborn—and almost every store we've opened since then—likened the look of our premises to an expensive hotel lobby or a casino.

Once you walk inside one of our stores, you know life is different because it doesn't at all resemble the typical British banking experience. Many British banks commit more than 50 percent of their retail space to ATMs because they don't want customers to talk to customer service representatives. We, on the other hand, want customers inside our stores, "safe, dry, and free." We want them on hand to see and enjoy the bank.

One day it was raining at the new Holborn store and we looked across the street and saw 20 people queuing up, in the rain, waiting to use an ATM outside a Sainsbury's supermarket. It made us crazy seeing their inconvenience when we had four ATMs indoors. We marched across the street with raincoats and umbrellas and escorted them back to our dry environs.

*

There are five major banks operating in the heart of London— Lloyds, Barclays, HSBC, NatWest, and RBS. They operate as any cartel would. They underserve, they overcharge, and they massively under-invest in their continuing business. They have a uniquely British philosophy that, "We're doing you a favor by letting you bank with us (or buy from us)."

I can tell you're already dubious—"There goes the disruptive American again!"

So let me back up the bold talk with a short overview of what we accomplished. (You'll learn the details—and be offered a model to follow in your own enterprise—in the chapters that follow.)

Growth

No one in the Western world has ever grown a retail bank 100 percent a year, compounded. Metro Bank did that in each of its first five years. And the number we use to make that point is that the average American bank branch grows deposits at a rate of $1 million per branch per year. Commerce grew $18 million annually, and Metro is growing $100 million per year, per store. No one—not in Britain, not in the United States—has ever created this kind of growth, whether in retail or banking. When we first opened, the volumes our stores attracted were scary to some. But our team quickly learned how to handle and master it.

Private Banking

We didn't have private banking to speak of at Commerce.

Private banking in the United States and in the United Kingdom meant two kinds of business. On the one hand, it was conventional banking and lending. On the other hand, it was asset management. The London banking cartel wanted to be in the asset management business. They *didn't* want to be in the banking business. They withdrew from the core business of banking—taking deposits and making loans—to try to attract these other businesses.

And we moved in.

Banking Service for Non-British Residents

Generally, British banks are afraid to open accounts for American individuals—no matter how rich or famous; you'd be astounded to learn who banks with us—or American businesses. And we are not afraid. We are actually *the* bank of the American government in London, too. It's a funny story, another example of where the British banking cartel went left and we've gone right. We love Americans; they're afraid of Americans.

Safe Deposit Boxes

It's crazy; we can't build or expand them fast enough in our London stores. In 2015, the London banking cartel shut down all safe deposit boxes in their bank branches. The incumbents owned 88 percent of the market when we arrived and by shutting down this aspect of service, they sent tens of thousands of customers racing into our arms.

Box fees alone now pay most of the rent for our stores, a category of income that wildly exceeded our original estimates. It's what I call found money. The cartel lost it; we found it.

*

At Metro Bank, it takes 15 minutes on average to open a new consumer account and 1 hour to open most new business accounts.

In summer 2015 that got us wondering: how long does it take for a business to open a new account with our traditional competitors, the cartel bankers?

We sent out mystery shoppers to "shop" our competition and put them to the test. (As you read this, consider how you stack up against your nearest competitors. Are you as good as you need to be? There's only one way to be sure.)

All our visits produced similar results. Our shoppers had a greater chance of being struck by lightning than actually seeing a business manager. *None* of the banks had greeters to welcome customers. None of the banks produced a business manager to discuss opening a new account; one Lloyds branch would bring one out only if we guaranteed "100%" to open the account—terms undisclosed—with them. None of the banks could set up a new business account the day we visited. Most referred us to telephone or online services or offered appointments one or more weeks in the future. In the branches where we were given the opportunity to leave our contact information for a follow-up call, no one ever followed up.

At Metro Bank, new business accounts usually open on the same day.

*

We set out to disrupt a large, established cartel market that takes customers for granted.

As far as the cartel banks are concerned, Metro Bank came to London from Mars. We went into a large market with five established banks that hadn't had a new competitor for 100-plus. They act like a cartel. They under-invest in the business. They overcharge. They underserve. Another word they use for it is oligarchy.

Not only did some of these banks fail during the crash, they also destroyed any relationship they had with their customers. And they absolutely take their customers for granted. We, by contrast, show up with a brand new, differentiated disruptor model, which says throw out all the established rules. Ignore what the competition has been doing; operate our *FANS not customers* brand.

We're also way ahead of everybody else on the tech side. The world has changed; while the store is our public face, the key element to success is that we deliver in every channel: bricks and mortar, online and mobile.

There are five gigantic banks in London. They've got

> **The Four Myths of UK Retail Banking**
>
> - No one switches accounts
> - Rate is everything
> - Banks make money only by cutting costs
> - The branch is dead

monumental problems, financial and operational. They almost can't be fixed. We are the least of their problems.

The most common question I get asked in London is this: how did you have the courage to come over here, knowing nobody, and start the first new bank in 170 years from scratch?

It was easy after I experienced the British banking customer service culture in person—and stopped laughing.

I told my wife, "Let's build the *real* deal."

As you read on in *FANS Not Customers*, we'll talk about why the Metro Bank model, imported from the United States, worked here. More importantly, we'll talk about how you can take your business model into a new market and make it work. Everything we did in New York works better here.*

*

No model works without colleagues who believe and execute. We have recruited thousands of colleagues—and will recruit thousands more in the future—and they have seen the magic of a unique culture executing the right model.

In the retail business there are companies that grow rapidly.

---

* Everything ... except the ATM machines. We put ATM machines inside the store foyers, where customers can be warm, dry, and safe. But the Brits voted with their feet: they would rather use them on the street, where they're cold, wet, and not safe.

They attract attention because they create excitement. People want to get a thrill out of patronizing your business, whether it's a bank, a retail store or even a pet insurance company.

Metro Bank is on its way toward creating fans and redefining British banking. And I can't wait to tell you how we do it.

Join the revolution!

2

Commerce Bank: Early Days, Winning Ways

I was an overnight success all right, but 30 years is a long, long night.

Ray Kroc, McDonald's

You must believe in your model.

Creating wealth is the result, not the objective, of what you do. I was always fascinated with business models—what's good and what's bad and why some succeed and others fail. And you often learn more from the ones that fail. What's the differentiator? Why does one succeed and another fail?

At one time in the US, McDonald's, Burger King and Burger Chef were all about the same size, and Burger Chef, which was owned by General Foods, had the deepest pockets. Yet Burger Chef was wiped off the face of the earth, and Burger King has been a weak second ever since. What is it about McDonald's that allowed it to come from a position of equal in the pack to be the dominant player? We see that in lots of business categories. What's the differentiator? Certainly, it's the people who manage a business, but it's always more than that.

It's something about the model that is different.

*

Commerce Bank opened its doors on June 29, 1973, in Marlton, New Jersey. It was a modest start, with just nine employees, one office, only $1.5 million of capital, and no brand. By 2007, it was a major American bank, growing at 23 percent per year. It went from being one of 24,000 community banks to being a regional powerhouse with a reputation for service on a par with McDonald's, Apple, and Starbucks.

Over 34 years, Shirley and I and a dedicated team of professionals built Commerce Bank from one location in southern New Jersey to 440 stores in six states with $50 billion in assets and $8 billion in market capitalization.

It proved to be a great investment. Anyone who invested $10,000 in Commerce Bank from the start, in 1973, would have seen their investment grow in value to $4.7 million in 2007. That's a 470 times increase, a 23 percent stock return compounded for 30 years.

We knew what we wanted to be, and we knew what we didn't want to be, and those lines just didn't cross. We were the attack model. What separated us was the dedication, the model, and the discipline to reinvent retail banking.

*

I am the oldest of six children. I grew up in Vienna, Virginia, a suburb of Washington, DC. As a teenager, I was always intrigued by the magic of business. I remember, in particular, an early fascination with the success of McDonald's and its ability to earn profits on a 15¢ hamburger.

From my high school days as a part-time bank employee, I was encouraged to pursue the banking business by my father, Vernon W. Hill. After focusing on residential real estate after World War II, Dad was involved with a group that started a small bank in Vienna. While working summer vacations there, I discovered an aptitude for it.

My father was an entrepreneur, self-employed for most of his life. And he bred—at least in me—an entrepreneurial zeal.

He always wanted a son of his to attend the University of Pennsylvania's Wharton School of Business. In 1963, since I was the oldest, I made my first trip north of Washington to the Penn campus, stuck around, and graduated from Wharton with a degree in economics in 1967.

While a student at Wharton, I also worked full-time in the banking industry, first for Philadelphia National Bank and later as a commercial lender at First Peoples Bank in southern New Jersey. The joke was you could not obtain a commercial mortgage in South Jersey before 12 noon "because Vernon is still in class."

My choices after graduating from Wharton included staying where I was or joining Irving Trust, a bank that offered me a management training position. Irving was located at One Wall Street (in 2005, Commerce Bank opened at Two Wall Street). I declined the offer, choosing South Jersey rather than the heart of Manhattan—real estate development rather than banking.

Following the entrepreneurial direction of my successful father, I created Site Development, a real estate development business focused on serving the needs of national retail clients. I was tasked with finding and developing new store sites for clients to approve. I got the sites. I was paid only for success.

My first client was McDonald's Corporation, for which our company developed sites throughout America. I even had the opportunity to personally show sites to the man who built McDonald's from a single location, Ray Kroc himself. Eventually, I developed 100-plus sites for McDonald's and 10 times as many for other companies.

In 1985, I partnered with Steven Lewis to acquire 25 Burger King restaurants in Pennsylvania, returning to my fast-food experience. Our partnership now operates more than 40 units in numerous states.

Banking, however, was always my first love and in 1972, at the age of 26, I gathered a small group of investors to raise the $1.5 million needed to obtain a new New Jersey bank charter. On June 29, 1973, Commerce Bank opened for business in Marlton, New Jersey, with one office and nine colleagues.

When we opened that first store, there were 24,000 separate banks in America. We were 24,001. How were we going to differentiate ourselves?

In our first year, we had a contest to give away an expensive red bicycle. It went on for a month, and every day one kid stuffed the ballot box—he filled out ten ballots a day. When we finally picked a winner, it was the kid. It *had* to be him. So we called and told him he had won. We were so excited for him—he really wanted that bike.

"Could I have the cash instead?" he said.

I was disappointed. We thought the kid couldn't afford a bike. I should have *recruited* him!

*

At Harvard, many years later, as we discussed the business school's Commerce Bank case study, I was asked by students about what kind of marketing research I did before choosing Commerce Bank's predominant and enduring color scheme— red. The answer: "Shirley and I laid out the newspapers on the floor," I said, "and found that no competitor used red. And so the Commerce (now Metro) 'Red' was born."

*

My wife and I are both Leos. You might wonder about how two lions could live under the same sign, but we each have different skill sets and the same appreciation and striving for perfection while working every day to make our lives and businesses better.

I remember that when Shirley first started her business, InterArch, she told my father how great it was going to be and what she had done to put it all in place. He seemed somewhat excited but then he said to her, "Come and see me in five years." Dad told Shirley that there's always an excitement about starting a business and that it breeds a kind of infectious enthusiasm. "We Americans love what's new," he said. "But in year two and three and four and 23 and 30, how do you get up every morning and keep it fresh and still look to improve?"

Fortunately, Shirley and I never lost the drive to keep our businesses—and our marriage—fresh.

*

I always believed that the world did not need another "Me, Too" anything, much less a bank. What is the value of a bank? It is found in its deposit base, which we grew with service. I set out to build a power retailing company modeled on the successful retailers of America rather than a typical bank.

McDonald's and Burger King influenced me, and I had been a fan before I was doing development for the former or a franchisee of the latter. Those experiences put me on a path to delivering a better banking experience.

A bank's business boils down to two sides: lending and deposits. It receives deposits and uses the same money to make loans. That's been the model for thousands of years. Lending, according to the conventional wisdom for centuries, was where value was created. Deposits were important, but lending was *more* important. The retail experience and customer service didn't account for much. The exceptions were community banks where deposits were their lifeblood.

Banking is, essentially, a government license to borrow money cheaply. Anyone can make loans, but only licensed, government-sanctioned banks can accept deposits. That's why the legal and economic value of a bank is in gathering deposits from loyal customers.

Could we really go head-to-head with the entire world and collect deposits? The influence of the retailing model meant that I approached the banking business by focusing first on gathering deposits, but then I adopted the best retail practices—not the best practices of banks. The smart move, over time, was more than attracting more deposits; it was bringing in a higher level of deposits at a lower cost. It's why you should build your own model around a unique advantage.

The secret of Commerce Bank—and now Metro Bank—was that not only did we have the most rapidly growing deposit base, we also had the lowest cost of deposit funding. The customer exchanged what they considered a better retail experience, of which ours was one, for a lower yield on their money—giving us more of their low-cost money. We competed on *service*—not price.

Commerce Bank was built on the theme of "America's Most Convenient Bank" and developed into one of the nation's most successful banks. In the beginning, Commerce had an original staff of nine with one office. By 2006, the bank had more than 14,000 employees with 440 offices in eight states and Washington, DC, and had redefined the banking business by delivering unsurpassed service and convenience.

In September 2001, Commerce made its debut in Manhattan with two stores. The bank eventually opened in 270 locations in metropolitan New York and attracted $25 billion in deposits, making metropolitan New York the largest Commerce market.

In mid-2005, Commerce began its expansion into the Metropolitan Washington, DC, market with ten stores. In early 2006, Commerce expanded its marketplace again by opening stores in Palm Beach County, Florida.

In 2007, Commerce Bank was sold to Toronto-based TD Bank for $8.5 billion, producing a 30-year, 23 percent annual shareholder return. Everyone profited, including shareholders and colleagues.

As *Forbes* reported in the 20–20–20 Club in 2006, only seven companies had a CEO serving 20-plus years with a 23 percent compounded return. We were proud to come fourth on that list, behind Lawrence J. Ellison (Oracle), Howard Solomon (Forest Labs) and Warren E. Buffett (Berkshire Hathaway).

*

As I went into new markets, from Philadelphia to Manhattan to London, the established local bankers told me that their market was different from all the others we were in and that our model had to be adapted to suit them. When I stopped hiring people who believed that, our machine started to work. If you have a successful model and you believe in it, it doesn't matter what the establishment says.

Our model was just as effective in North Jersey or downtown Philly or DC or Manhattan, or even in London. We made up our minds that we wanted local people with local flavor in each market—running *our* model.

Commerce Bank hit multiple walls along the way to $50 billion in assets and $8.5 billion in market value. We had to evolve, our management had to evolve, the capabilities of our people had to evolve and grow. If we hadn't evolved, we would have become road kill.

And now we have found another market, London, where our unique model also adds tremendous customer and shareholder value, and where we will continue to evolve.

As you create your own unique model, you, your management and the model need to continually grow and improve. Your choices are to improve and grow or calcify and die.

My View
Tom Brown
Founder, Bankstocks.com

In 1998, I was reading the *Wall Street Journal*, and there was this front page story about a bank that I had never heard of in New Jersey and how successful they were and how different they were from everybody else, because they were opening branches like crazy when everybody else was closing them.

It was Commerce Bank.

They didn't care if the customers had different levels of profitability and that some customers were unprofitable, they served everybody equally. They offered extended hours in their branches, their cost of doing business was high, when the rest of the banks that I was looking at were lowering their cost of delivery, so everything that I thought was going to lead to being a winner, Commerce was doing just the opposite.

I was at Tiger Management at the time, and I called up the bank and asked to speak to the CEO. Much to my surprise, not now but then, Vernon Hill took the call. We spent maybe an hour and a half on the phone. He was telling me about the bank and concluded with, "You really should come down here and see us." Soon I met with him in his office, and he said, "Let's go out and visit some of these stores." That was an eye-opening experience for me, and it really changed the way I looked at what it was going to take to be successful in retail banking. In fact, a lot of what I thought banks would be able to execute, they weren't able to do. It was too complicated. Systems didn't talk to each other. Meanwhile, Commerce was knocking the cover off the ball.

One of the things that I enjoy is a good spar. Vernon does, too, so it was a match made in heaven between the two of us. We had a great discussion.

What was incredibly unusual was that the CEO would drive me around to individual branches. The CEOs at most of the companies that I looked at didn't even know where their branches were. Another CEO would never know anybody inside that branch, so all of this was different. The other thing that he did was point out competitor branches along the way.

Most of the CEOs of big banks do not come from the retail side of the business. Most came from the corporate side of business, so there was, until 2000, inattention to the retail side.

In banking, there is certainly an over-emphasis on not failing. Don't do something different if you might fail at it. Vernon has not been afraid. One of the most important elements of his success is that he has not been afraid to try things that either nobody else does or that conventional wisdom says is wrong.

At our firm, we do what is called an annual "Branch Hunt." That's where we divide up into teams, and we walk down each of the avenues on the East Side of Manhattan. Everybody is given about $500, and they are told that they have to open two current accounts at two different institutions. They check out every financial institution. If they don't open two current accounts, they give the money back, and nobody has ever given me any money back. At the end of the branch hunt, we all get together and tell our stories and show our pictures, and that was when it became hilarious how poor the execution of everybody else was compared with Commerce. There was this woman that helped us at Commerce. I said, "How did you find Commerce?" She said, "I moved here from South America, and I was working for a dentist. I asked the dentist, 'Where should I open a checking account?' He said, 'Commerce Bank, because they work late hours, and they are open late, and it would be very convenient.'" So she opened up her current account there, and she was so impressed with the people that she quit her job as a dental assistant and went to work for Commerce Bank.

I think Shirley, Vernon's wife, was the secret weapon of Commerce Bank and is exactly that now at Metro Bank. She is the keeper of the brand, produces design as a competitive weapon, and enforces the culture.

I was in Atlanta and one of my meetings was at SunTrust, which is one of the top ten banks in the US. I was listening to them talk about how they're changing their approach to retail and it got me thinking about the old Commerce model. The thing about the old Commerce model that, frankly, Vernon and I disagreed with each other on was that if I asked him, "What's the key to the system?" he would say, "The system!" I would say it was the branch manager and I still felt that when I was listening to how SunTrust was redefining the job of the branch manager; then I thought of the branch managers that participated in the old Commerce system.

They were disproportionately women. They were anywhere from 35 to 60 years of age and the big difference between them and their competitors was, number one, that the women *owned* their branch. They'd do the branch's deposit totals and they were the number one small business banker for that branch. By the way, these women—mostly women, there were some men— were happy being a branch manager and they weren't viewing it as a stepping-stone. You literally could go across the street to a PNC branch or what's now a Wells Fargo branch and you'd see a 20-something-year-old male running the branch and they wouldn't want to be there. They were doing this, they hoped, for two years and then they'd be on to something else.

The women managers, on the other hand, liked the flexibility of hours, the fact it was close to home, that they were serving their friends. Most of the branch managers in the Commerce system were very local. You wouldn't necessarily find that in the biggest banks.

It was fun when Vernon would take me in his car and we'd go to Commerce branches and we'd go to competitors and what was striking was who these people were at his branches and how they knew their numbers and how *Vernon* knew their numbers. There were very few metrics that they focused on, so the key metric was, "What are my deposits?"

And then we'd go by the competitors' branches and notice how the larger competitors got their branches primarily through acquisition as opposed to construction. I remember one where I couldn't even tell it was a Wachovia branch.

Vernon reinvented American retail banking. His focus on service created a true growth retailer. No one else has grown an American bank internally at 23 percent per year for 30-plus years. *No one.*

Part 2

Marketing is *Everything*

3

Fans Not Customers

The greatest luxury is time, and service can help you
make the most of that. Give greater productivity, greater
enjoyment—what better luxury can there be?

Isadore Sharp, founder, Four Seasons Hotels and Resorts

Customers are those people who bank with us but who are not
yet emotionally attached.

They're drawn by proximity and by the convenience model.
They are indifferent at the beginning; they are customers. We
are perfectly happy having customers.

But we want to convert them to *fans*.

Fans are customers who become part of our community,
remain loyal, and convert their friends to new customers of our
brand.

Fans add a new dimension, as in when somebody is whing-
ing about their bank or some banking tactic, and they jump in
to say, "Oh, go to Metro, that's *my* bank!"

Or they will see someone from our team, away from the
bank, wearing a bright red Metro "M" pin, and start a conversation with a total stranger. "You work for Metro Bank? That's *my*
bank. I love that bank."

When people talk about our bank like that, it's because we created a fan as opposed to a customer.

If you aren't doing business with Metro Bank yet, you're probably scoffing at this as malarkey: "It's a bank, for heaven's sake!" Banking is a commodity, after all. One is just like the next and the next." (And Apple is just a computer company!) But fans sing our praises to their neighbors, to co-workers, to someone they don't know sitting on the tube seat next to them.

Fifty percent of any company's business probably comes from family and friends sharing its praises: "I love that company." That's the difference between screaming, raving fans and mere customers. Customers are indifferent. They like Metro Bank, but they might never endorse us in a public place. But the more fans you have, it's like dispatching evangelists or disciples to sell your product.

The result of building fans was the internal deposit growth at Commerce Bank of 23 percent a year, compounded over 30 years.

Every great business will build fans.

*

How do we create fans?

A man came into a Metro Bank store one evening and left his cheque book on his customer service representative's desk. After he left, the CSR saw it, got his name and account, checked his identification and gave him a ring on his mobile. It was after 8pm and the store was closed. The customer was relieved to know his financial information was secure and figured he'd come in the next day to collect it. But our CSR said, "Tell me where you are." It was 8.30pm and he was at a pub about ten minutes away with friends. The CSR said, "I walk past there on my way home. I'll pop in and drop it off." He went into the pub and found the customer sitting around a table with ten friends.

The CSR walked over and returned the cheque book. Not long after, the CSR received an email saying, "Thank you! All my friends were blown away and they're all going to come and open accounts because that was just so amazing."

Nobody said to the CSR, "Do that." It's not something that will ever be found in an employee manual. That's just somebody doing the right thing. And that simple kindness created a fan within that person and ten more potential fans because their friend blurted out, "Wasn't that amazing?"

More stories that illustrate the *FANS not customers* point:

- A customer visited the Staines store to make two international payments and mentioned her family was waiting for her at a restaurant. A Metro cashier processed the payments while the customer went on to dinner, and personally took the paperwork to her so she could sign the payment. The customer came in the next day to open Young Savers accounts for each of her children.

- A mother and her young son visited our Tottenham Court Road store to open a Young Savers account for the little boy and a current account and safe deposit box for mum. One of our CSRs kept the little boy entertained at the Magic Money Machine while his mother opened the accounts. Later in the day, a lead cashier and CSR saw that the little boy had left his hat behind. The Metro staffers delivered the hat back to the boy. His mother said the hat had sentimental value, and was given to her son as a Christmas present by his great-uncle, who sadly passed away a few weeks later.

- Teachers from Bromley visited our store there with six shopping bags full of coins that their students had collected. They needed the coins counted, exchanged for notes, and ready for a school assembly that afternoon. Unfortunately, the Magic Money Machine stopped working, so a store manager and CSR drove the coins to our nearest store, in Orpington, and finished the job there. They personally drove to the school to make sure the students received the money in time.

- A customer visited the Staines store and ordered a fixed term deposit certificate that they desperately needed. Instead of making the customer wait for the certificate in the post, cashiers hand-delivered it to the grateful customer's home.

- At our Milton Keynes Midsummer store, a customer asked for directions to the coach station. A CSR not only provided directions, he also walked him to the ATM and called a taxi for the customer, who was carrying several bags. The CSR asked him for his account number. As he helped the gentlemen to the taxi, he explained that he had popped some money into his account to cover the cost of the taxi.

If UK banks that aren't named Metro have fans, we haven't heard about it. I have a few friends who don't bank with us, for reasons like location or rate. But I won't provide them with a better rate just to get their account. I enjoy hearing them whinge about the awful service they endure and remind them that, for example, an extra 0.25 percent in interest must be worth their time.

Career bankers recognize their distinct lack of loyal fans. *I* know that *they* know they don't deserve it.

*

Emotional brands create massive value; building *FANS not customers* creates emotional brands.

There are different kinds of brands. There's the basic brand where the name relates to a product. There are other brands

where you feel good about them. But there are legendary brands where the experience overwhelms the product and those brands create fans. And, of course, Apple continues to be the best example of this.

The fast-food model influenced much of what we do at Metro Bank, from making all channels accessible to consumers, to saturating communities with stores for their convenience and treating every customer, large or small, like royalty.

The Home Depot, under its co-founders, Bernie Marcus and Arthur Blank, was a company that inspired a legion of loyal, devoted fans. Men gave up their neighborhood hardware stores in droves to go to a place that excelled at carrying every product that they could possibly imagine they needed and more they never even dreamed of but with which they still fell in love. And they made shopping fun.

We want evangelists for our brand. We want brand ambassadors who spread the word about us, people who are passionate about us as a company because we've exceeded their expectations at every contact and opportunity. Every person we recruit, every person who works for our companies, passionately believes in not just doing an okay job, but doing the best possible job they can and creating the best customer experience they can.

I believe that all customers have value; most bankers will tell you that only their biggest depositors and borrowers are important. Metro Bank treats everyone equally well.

Our job and our responsibility are to make an emotional connection with our customers first, but then to go above and beyond, exceeding their expectations when it comes to customer service, so they become fans. Customers will show up and dutifully do business with us. But *fans* will tell their friends and neighbors about Metro Bank, helping us grow our company because of their personal satisfaction.

We have never fired anybody for giving too much service. That will never happen.

In London, where customer service expectations in banks are so low, one of our CSRs started talking to a man about his background and where he grew up. Small talk, but he was so impressed by her genuine interest that he burst into tears of happiness in the store. He said that no one working in a bank had ever wanted to know that much about him.

We installed safe deposit boxes in Britain just like we did in America, thinking it was no big deal. Activity was steady, if unspectacular. Then the big four cartel banks, with complete disregard for their clients, said safe deposit boxes were too much trouble and shut them all down, and told their customers they had a month to remove theirs. This reinforced their disdain for their customers. Subsequently, we were overwhelmed by safe deposit box demand. We increased the supply in every store. Today, our safe deposit box rental income almost exceeds our store rental expense.

Our first stores came with 600 safe deposit boxes. But we

underestimated the demand, and as the other banks abruptly eliminated their own safe deposit services, we adjusted our minimum installation to 1,200 boxes per store. Most have more; we put 4,000 safe deposit boxes in Southall alone.

If Shirley has to find space for more after a store is open, she will design a double vault.

She had lunch with Benita Refson, a founder of the British children's charity Place2Be (which is officially supported by the Duchess of Cambridge).

Barclay's Bank, which had been Benita's bank for 20-plus years, sent her a letter shortly before they had lunch that said: "Come and get your safe deposit box."

Shirley said, "Benita, where do you keep it now?"

"It's behind a sofa in my husband's office," she said. "I don't know what to do with it."

"Would you like a box at Metro Bank?" Shirley asked.

"Yes."

Shirley picked up her phone and called the manager of the Metro Bank store that was most convenient for Benita. The manager sent the papers to her office for signature and she had a new box by the day's end—and we had a new customer. And a new fan.

*

Sometimes, in addition to simply helping a customer open a new account, we might give them a tour of the store. In so doing, we can explain why we do things the way we do, demonstrating in words and deeds what services will be available to them.

We'll walk customers over to the Magic Money Machine and point out that it will count their coins for free and provide a voucher that can be exchanged for cash. The Magic Money Machines are for adults and children alike. You'll find one in each of our stores ready to count your saved coins. They're free to use and great fun if you want to guess the value of your coins with our interactive game—you could even win a prize.

Our machines sort the coins for you so you don't need to, and there's no limit to the value of coins you can bring in—a great excuse to save more.

*

Here are some more fans' experience stories from Metro Bank stores:

- An elderly woman said she hated doing business with plastic cards and much preferred cheques. We told her that we printed both in our stores. That weekend, she transferred her accounts—totaling £250,000—from her previous bank to ours all because she kept running out of cheques and we printed new ones in the store.

- A customer lost his wallet out of town and was stuck. He rang us up and said, "I really have a problem here. I've lost my wallet. I can't get a train ticket. I can't get home. What can you do?" We checked his account and he had plenty of money in it. We rang the ticket office in Reading where he was sitting. We paid for his ticket over the phone. That was all done by somebody at AMAZE Direct, our call center. We knew nothing about it until he came in the next day and told a manager that the experience was "Genuinely amazing!"

At other British financial institutions, just to put these events in perspective, most employees wouldn't have even thought of taking any of these extra steps. They have processes to follow and the processes are considered more important than actually thinking. It wouldn't have entered their minds, whereas we encourage our colleagues to act independently and in the moment. We give them the stories and tell them this is what we empower them to do. Anywhere else, the team member at the call center would have probably been told off for taking too long on her calls—it took 40 minutes to get the stranded customer a ticket and get him to the right booth to collect it. *We* made a big fuss about it: we made that team member a star.

Here is another example.

When we discover somebody opening a new account on their birthday we'll often round up several CSRs and sing an impromptu "Happy Birthday" just to make them feel special.

It's instilling these behaviors in our colleagues that really makes the difference between Metro Bank and the "Me, Too" bank across the street. I'm a firm believer that anybody can copy your products. Anybody can copy your hours, your colors and your money handling policies, but they cannot copy your culture because that is the very fabric of who you are and why you are different. We are defined by the way we answer customer questions, the way we give them accurate and timely information, and the way we make sure that they leave very, very happy.

One of the unique characteristics of Metro Bank is that everybody works together. There are no silos and no agendas. We stand shoulder to shoulder, aligned for the good of the customer, for the good of the bank.

Our never-ending goal is to surprise and delight.

*

We grew Commerce Bank's commercial business every year. There were many reasons for that. We went out and saw our customers face-to-face. We went to their places of business. We wanted to know who they were, where they've been, where they are, and where they want to go. We strove to understand their business goals and plans. And just as important, we wanted them to understand us. This was pure relationship banking. We never did deals for the sake of doing the deal, no matter how good the loan might have been.

When the bank started, potential customers no doubt compared our offerings on a simple level: "I want the best rate." And we didn't always win them over in a side-by-side comparison of our interest rate on savings with a bank in the cartel. But now that they've seen Metro Bank in operation—either as fans or someone who knows a happy fan—they have a better appreciation for the incomparable service we offer.

We could have been very opportunistic, saying, "This is your rate, and you can't get that anywhere else." But that would have sat uneasily with us. All the customers we've helped over the past few years—as the cartel banks repaired their balance sheets and dropped loans off their books—now see us with fresh eyes. The cartel banks are racing to the bottom on how low they can go on rates. It's fantastic, because we're not going anywhere near that.

Rate is what the big banks are using as a tool to get back into the market because their brands have been through trauma; their *only* way to compete today is on rate—in other words, price. But what does their brand stand for? We compete on *service.*

If an account officer goes to a customer's workplace with their Metro Bank boss—or sometimes even with the bank president or CEO—it builds the relationship like nothing else. Customers love it when we visit them at their place of business. They love it when senior management takes an interest.

When Metro Bank officers have a big loan that needs senior approval from headquarters, they tell their customer that it has to be reviewed by Craig or Vernon. Their reaction isn't, "Who are those guys?" because they probably already know at least one of us. Customers in every market have a chance to meet our senior executives and develop a personal relationship. Where else in Britain except Metro Bank can the customers meet the founder or the CEO? Nobody here has ever seen a bank CEO in a branch before.

Our local directors—store managers, in retail parlance—are the face of Metro Bank in each local market. They know the lawyers, doctors, shopkeepers, and restaurateurs in the neighborhood or town; they know their accounts. If anything moves in their community, they make sure Metro is the first bank to be in contact with another bank's existing customer or an existing Metro customer with growth plans to see how we can help them.

It's a great job for ambitious men and women because, while the cartel banks are so internally focused, they don't even know we are out talking to—and flirting with—their customers. We talk to non-customers more than their own bank talks to them. The local directors' job is to win business from the competition, again and again. And it isn't that complicated, because the big banks are badly serving these customers, many of which are great businesses that are desperate for capital to grow. It might be a credit policy issue or a cultural issue.

Our clients love the fact that their local Metro Bank director is responsible for everything in their area. They are the local banker. It doesn't matter if it is a private banking customer or a commercial customer. The bottom line is you're a *Metro* customer. We will look after you and help you as best we can.

These relationships reinforce the unparalleled quality of our loan portfolio. They put us in a position to react quickly to our customers' credit needs. They put us in a position where, if a customer is having a hiccup with their business, they don't run and hide from us. They come in and talk to us, and they say, "Look, I've got a little problem. Here's what I need. Here's what I can do for you in the meantime in the way of more collateral or more guarantee," and we can and will work through the problem.

The other benefit of our relationships is that these same

customers love referring their own clients and suppliers to us. We build the bulk of our business in that way. It is *real* relationship banking.

My View
Colum Smith
CEO, McMillan Williams Solicitors
I am a lawyer with ideas for expanding my legal practice that are considered unusual by my profession.

Vernon Hill gave me some of his time. He looked at my business model, told me what I needed to do, told me why this would work or wouldn't work in the financial world. He told me how to raise money and what the disadvantages would be.

Using that knowledge, I went off and became one of the few private equity backed law firms in the UK.

Why did I seek his advice? Because Vernon did what I wanted to do on a much bigger scale, in America, and now he's repeating it here. He's already been successful. And he learned from whatever errors he made the first time round, so he will be even more successful with Metro. With him, I can tap into, what, 40 years' worth of experience to avoid making the cockups? That seemed to be a blindingly obvious thing to do.

Another thing we took from Vernon was keeping the brand the same across the enterprise, because there aren't many legal brands in the UK. So everything we do is the same from office to office. The chairs are the same, the carpet is the same, the frontage is the same. Everyone wears an "MW" badge, just as everyone at Metro wears an "M" button. I don't know any other law firms that do anything like that. What if lawyers don't want to wear a badge? We don't care. What we want is an introduction that leads to more clients. It's just another way in.

We have shamelessly ripped Vernon off by copying him. If you go to the high street in three or four years' time, there will be more than 100 MW offices, all labeled exactly the same, all looking exactly the same, all offering the same product mix, all with the central support. There's nobody else doing that in the UK in law.

The key aspect was becoming customer-centric, dealing with complaints, protecting our brand, thinking big. Vernon told me, "Think big—think national; don't think local. Plan national from the beginning. Don't plan local. Otherwise, you'll be knocking down what you've spent time building. Bring in bigger people."

Before I met Vernon, I didn't know I was operating a disruptive model because I'm not a businessman, I'm a lawyer. I simply said, "This is what I'm going to do." To which Vernon said, "That's a disruptive business model; just like Metro is a disruptive business model."

I give lots of speeches and I give credit where credit's due— to Metro. People will raise a hand and ask, "How did you know their business model was going to work for you?" And I say, "If it works for Metro, why wouldn't it work for me? I discussed it with Mr Hill himself." And at that point, they shut up, because who wants to be critical of a man who made that much money? I wouldn't advise it. You'd look like an idiot.

4

Putting the "Grand" in Grand Openings

> If I had a brick for every time I've repeated the phrase
> Quality, Service, Cleanliness and Value, I think I'd probably
> be able to bridge the Atlantic Ocean with them.
>
> Ray Kroc, founder, McDonald's

For months, as we constructed the first Metro Bank, the average Londoner passing our Holborn location couldn't begin to guess what was going on behind the 15-foot tall windows facing out onto the street. They were teased with a simple, unfamiliar, and unlikely sentiment: "Love Your Bank At Last."

At a time when no British high street banking establishment enjoyed an inspiring customer satisfaction rating—and, in fact, most were under 20 percent—the idea that anyone in the UK could love a bank seemed absurd.

More than 100,000 people a day went past those windows, thanks to their proximity to Holborn tube station. It was a joke to some, a mystery to others. Newspapers and TV news reports picked up on the signs and did frequent updates on our progress, talking about these "crazy people" who want to start a new bank.

Needless to say, we were discouraged from hosting live

bands, stilt walkers and free food. But we stuck to our guns and proceeded with the first Metro Bank grand opening circus.

The Americans in our operation were cautious about misinterpreting and underestimating the cultural differences between the Yanks and the Brits. We were getting good advance press, but what if nobody showed up?

Two days before we opened, that fear was allayed. A producer from the BBC One "Breakfast" show called and asked, "Can we broadcast our morning show live from Holborn during your grand opening?" (This was the equivalent of NBC's "Today" show making a similar request in the US.)

We said, "Yes," of course, and amid all our other preparations, added a layer of staff to work with the TV crew's 4am arrival to prepare for a 6–9am live telecast from inside the first Metro Bank store.

The night before, we decided not to take any chances on opening and nobody showing up. We asked our property agent to come in that morning and officially open an account on camera and asked the entire opening day staff to give similar invitations to friends and family. "We've got to have people at the front door, queuing up, at 8am. What if we're on the BBC and nobody shows up?"

It was a fail-safe move, and in retrospect it seems silly to have wasted energy worrying about it. But our trepidation the night before was palpable.

What did happen that morning was that BBC One was simply the TV network that phoned ahead for permission to broadcast from our site; in total, media from 12 different countries showed up, sending reporters to interview, shoot video, record audio and take photographs. There were British, European, Australian, American, Japanese and even North Korean TV production trucks lining the streets, all sent to do a story on a bank opening in London! That's how bad the existing British banking industry's reputation had become.

Customers poured in but they barely outnumbered the reporters and camera operators. Thank goodness the live BBC One broadcast encouraged more people to come out and experience Metro Bank in person.

Meanwhile, we opened accounts on the spot, instantly issuing debit cards and credit cards—something unheard of in London, where customers typically wait several weeks for an appointment just to apply to a bank for a new account, then wait a couple of weeks more to be approved to join their exclusive club and get their card and PIN in the post. There were bands playing outside, where Shirley and I greeted prospective customers alongside our Yorkshire terrier Duffy, who welcomed their dogs, as well as colorful stilt walkers and beaming colleagues who distributed free food (including 8,000 bags of popcorn) and drinks, balloons, shoe shines and manicures.

"We were overwhelmed by the customer response," CEO Craig Donaldson said later.

The Holborn store has a grand staircase and, from its top, we looked out on the street and witnessed waves of humanity. You'd think The Beatles had reunited and were expected to arrive at any moment!

It was glorious mayhem. And that was just the *first* day. The grand opening continued for three days, but the atmosphere of excitement and magic continues to this day.

*

On the night of the grand opening we had planned a dinner at the Gherkin (the former site of the Baltic Exchange, at 30 St Mary Axe, which acquired its unofficial name because the building is pickle-shaped) as a celebration for investors, board members and some Metro Bank executives. As it turned out, no executives made it because they were still serving new customers.

*

Every new Metro Bank store celebrates its opening in similarly grand style for two full days, Friday and Saturday.

We blitz the area for two weeks before, handing out cards that invite the bearer to switch their account to Metro Bank. We also tell them to bring the family and even the dog—everybody is welcome at the party.

The excitement starts in earnest on the previous Wednesday with a VIP party for neighboring businesses and politicians in selected locations. Thursday is for stocking the store with food and new customer gifts, followed by the grand opening hoopla on Friday and Saturday. We're open seven days a week, so that first weekend is rounded out by a soft Sunday to get ready for the first full week of business and to welcome pleasantly surprised customers who aren't expecting to find a neighborhood bank open on the seventh day.

The big openings started in the earliest days of Commerce Bank because we were going into new locations all the time where people didn't know us. It's a great way to make a splash. The event announces to the local community, "This isn't what you'd normally expect of a bank!" It speaks to our policy of "exceed expectations" and "surprise and delight" in every way possible.

Why do we make grand openings such a production? That's easy: first impressions are lasting. The elements that create a spectacular launch are basically what the brand offers and how well it is executed. Our grand openings are almost like putting together a Broadway or West End show. Everyone has a role, from store captains and section leaders to runners. When the doors open to the public, everyone is well rehearsed and knows exactly what they are to do; no one deviates from that. Execution is everything.

For example, we don't want customer service representatives—whose primary job during a new store opening is to set

The Media React to the Grand Opening of Metro Bank UK

"Metro Bank is a force for banking good ... Metro Bank is something to sing about."

Jeff Prestridge, *Daily Mail*, March 18, 2011

"As far as *This Is Money* knows, walking out at Holborn station on a Thursday morning doesn't usually involve dodging blue and red clad women wobbling around on stilts, shoe shiners, a live jazz band or feeding biscuits to excitable dogs."

Tara Evans, *This Is Money*, August 2, 2010

"Upstart shakes up banking sector with full service on Sunday."

Phillip Inman, *Guardian*, August 1, 2010

"Shoppers piling out of Holborn tube station on their way to Covent Garden today will be greeted by an unusual sight: a bank open for business on a Sunday."

Jill Treanor, *Observer*, August 1, 2010

"Amidst the razzmatazz of balloons and a trad jazz band playing outside, I found real interest from the first customers, not just idle curiosity."

Ian Pollock, BBC News, July 29, 2010

"Metro Bank will focus on Greater London for its first ten years. Now that it has opened it raises a rather obvious question ... Why hasn't anyone thought of doing this before?"

Ian Pollock, BBC News, July 29, 2010

"Metro Bank opens on Sunday as battle for high street hots up."

Jill Treanor, *Observer*, August 1, 2010

"Ready to do business: first high street bank in 100 years opens its doors (and will only shut them four days a year)."

Sean Poulter, *Daily Mail*, July 30, 2010

"This was no ordinary Thursday morning. It was the grand opening of the UK's first start up bank in over 100 years, Metro Bank, and they sure had put on a show."

Tara Evans, *This Is Money*, August 2, 2010

"Metro Bank looks like it could be up to the task, putting excellent customer service at the top of its agenda."

Jane Baker, Lovemoney.com, July 29, 2010

"Hundreds of customers flocked to Holborn yesterday after the first high street bank to launch in Britain for more than 100 years opened its doors."

Jamie Dunkley, *Daily Telegraph*, July 29, 2010

up new accounts—to waste time because something they need isn't at hand. We have what we call "runners", whose sole task is to be close by to get whatever the CSR needs to stay fully involved with the prospective new customer. When a deposit has to be made, we have prearranged signals for runners to come to the desk and pick up a deposit.

Team leaders wear headsets and are assigned sections of the store to monitor. If there is a question or an issue, or an approval is needed, that's a "bump it up." The bump it up person will come over and do their best to say "Yes" to whatever the customer needs.

The back room is crucial during a grand opening to make sure that deposits are processed appropriately and quickly; that all the necessary paperwork gets done correctly; that proper identification is taken.

It's complicated. We hold grand opening training sessions so there are few surprises for even the greenest of colleagues and they know exactly what to do and how to do it. It's really something to see. Colleagues from already open stores always help staff these sunup-to-sundown events, providing experience—and relief—to new associates. (And it doesn't hurt ambitious colleagues to see and be seen by the bank's leadership.)

There are greeters at the door to welcome everyone who comes in and a waiting-list host or hostess who manages the flow so that no one queues unnecessarily. If there is a wait of any kind, we will give the customer a coupon to get a cup of coffee nearby at Eat or Pret a Manger, and we'll hand out a beeper that will signal it's time to return and open an account.

The grand opening is extremely important to our brand because we're welcoming the community to come into our store and bank with us. We want their experience to be different and better than anywhere else that they have ever been.

Often we'll hire performing dogs, which are guaranteed to draw a crowd. We have people outside the store who we call "blitzers"; they hand out red Metro Bank balloons to children, put Metro Bank bandanas on dogs, and generally engage people to come on in and see what we're about.

Every great company includes a "fun" element in its model that engages and enthralls its customers with never-ending surprise and delight.

Celebrate your openings, celebrate your new customers. And celebrate that you are becoming part of a new community. If you make it an event, if you *believe* it is an event, your customers will, too.

5

The New Maths

I am not making watches only to look at the time. I am making jewels! They are jewels!

Nicolas Hayek, founder, Swatch

Every decision you make will strengthen or weaken your brand. In the long term, a reinforcing client base is more important than earnings in the next quarter.

The Metro formulas are:

The Metro Bank Model + Our AMAZE(ING) Culture + Fanatical Execution = FANS

Retail + Entertainment = Metro Bank

Great Ideas + Excellent Execution = The Never-ending Story

Let's examine each one individually.

The Metro Bank Model + Our AMAZE(ING) Culture + Fanatical Execution = FANS

The Metro Bank model requires that, as a power retailer, we exceed our customers' expectations every day by providing superior products, services, facilities, and delivery channels.

Converting words into action happens via our specially designed stores and branded colors, and features extended hours, seven-day-a-week availability, unique personalized service, application of the latest technology, and no-fee policies that enable Metro Bank to turn customers into fans with a unique banking experience and to grow deposits at reliable, steady rates.

Differentiating the Metro Bank model is its:

- focus on deposits;
- extra, added customer value;
- an unmatched retail experience, always;
- unparalleled facilities in the most desirable location;
- the best of every delivery channel;
- the end of traditional stupid bank rules;
- a revenue growth model, not a cost-cut model.

The Metro brand is the essence of Metro Bank's identity. Metro customers know and expect nothing less, making it Metro's top asset.

We see our main responsibility thus:

- **Protect the brand**—*do nothing stupid*!
- **Refine the brand**—*make it better all the time*!
- **Expand the brand**—*find new products and new areas where we can add value*!

Culture is the social fabric of Metro Bank—its DNA. Culture matches the store's model and is the lifeblood of the organization.

Culture can't be merged, culture can't be acquired, and culture can't be converted. The essence of Metro Bank is its combination of a distinct model and a culture that is reinforced daily.

We have consistently followed the same model and strategy across four decades and two continents. It's the Metro Bank heritage.

The customer comes first at all costs, as will the profitability from the adventure this brings. The "street" bankers we seek out embrace that culture and hustle for new business every minute of every day.

When I ask something of a Metro Bank colleague, such as "Get the new store open in four days," the response is straight forward: "I'll *find* a way to do it."

The words "I can't" are not spoken around here.

From Metro branded balloons and clothing to our Metro Man mascot, Metro Bank colleagues share their joy and pleasure in taking great customer service to new levels.

We call our intense dedication to exceeding customers' expectations our "AMAZE! the Customer" philosophy. Metro Bank University, our employee education center, immerses our colleagues in the AMAZE! the Customer culture from day one.

Any business can boast a great model with a reinforcing culture, but execution will determine its ultimate fate. Great retailers know that what happens at the store level—at the point of customer contact—and not at the corporate level, will determine the fate of a company. Retail is *detail.*

Fanatical business execution requires:

- belief in your model;
- over-investment in facilities and people;
- full and complete execution.

Our regional market management system provides a differentiated customer experience at every point of contact, backed by the technological and financial strength of a financial services company with incredible growth. The strength of the Metro Bank model leads us to over-invest in people, training and facilities.

Retail + Entertainment = Metro Bank

Two things stood out to me as I studied the history of retailing as a young businessman:

1. No legendary retailer was ever created through acquisitions. All the top household names did it by experimenting, configuring a model that could survive, refining it, and then expanding it. You only have to be 15 percent better than the retail competition in order to beat them, and you must improve all the time. At Metro Bank, we will never be happy with what we have; we insist on getting better and better.

2. There are few or no examples of broken big retail models that have ever been fixed. The urban landscape is littered with their tragic failures. When you get past the point of broken people, procedures, facilities, and delivery, customers can see your model is broken, and that's impossible to fix. They won't wait, either; there is too much quality competition for their money.

I agree with most people who look around and think there are a lot of banks in the world—probably too many undifferentiated commodity banks and "Me, Too" models. Success for us and you is about creating and delivering differentiated, value-added, fun business experiences.

Legendary retailers create fun experiences for their customers, turning them into fans. The banking business doesn't have to be dull. Our Metro Magic Money Machines are fun and appeal to children and adults alike. Bring your dog into any Metro Bank store and it will find a biscuit, a water dish and a Metro Bank scarf awaiting it. For kids, there are bright red lollipops. The lighting is bright and the atmosphere vibrant.

Great Ideas + Excellent Execution = The Never-ending Story

In most large companies there are various silos reporting to chief officers of compliance, marketing, operations, and audit, and each has a point of view that reflects their fiefdom. But what do their individual concerns do to the brand they all represent?

There is a NatWest bank branch next door to the Metro store in Uxbridge, west London. During the first day of our two-day grand opening celebration, NatWest put out a sign-board in front of their store that said, "NatWest customers, we are thinking about extending our hours." It didn't say that they would do it—or when!

Another NatWest office *did* open on a Saturday to compete with us, but they would not allow banking transactions. So why were they open? Beats us!

One of the other high street banks extended its hours during the 2012 Olympics, but once the Olympics ended, so did the extended hours.

Another anti-customer behavior we observed was that *many London banks ended their safe deposit box services*. Considering the nonsensical way most British banks offered the service in the first place, this might not have been a bad idea. We, on the other hand, serve success.

In the US, almost every bank offers secure safe deposit box services. Boxes come in standardized sizes—small, medium and large—provided by the bank. Usually two keys are required to unlock them: one kept by the customer, the other by the bank. And they are stored in a vault that is sealed when the bank is not open.

In the UK, we observed a very different approach. If you want a safe deposit box, you have to buy your own at a hardware store. It could be metal, plastic or even cardboard. It could lock—or not. And where does the bank store it? Heaven knows.

My wife and I opened a safe deposit box at the Barclays

branch down the street from the Metro Bank in Hounslow, west London. We wanted to test the British system and went to the bank to retrieve something from our box.

First, good luck getting help from a customer "service" rep. Our request was met with eye rolls and sighs as we were handed from one unhelpful employee to another. And we still have no idea where our box was stored because they wouldn't tell or show us.

While many British banks were writing off this service, we recognized it as an enormous business opportunity. The Asian community is especially enamored of safe deposit boxes in the UK and the US. (In New York at Commerce Bank and in London at Metro Bank, we installed thousands of boxes in stores in neighborhoods with large Asian populations.)

British bank employees don't appear to trust each other, so management can't send just one person to retrieve a box. And because there are many different sizes and types of boxes, it takes these people forever to find the right one. We've also heard numerous reports of lost boxes.

When you finally complete your business and return the box, the bank employees roll their eyes again and sometimes shove your box of valuables on the floor underneath the counter until someone can be bothered to put it away "properly."

And just in case our experience was unique, we sent Metro Bank employees to five more high street banks with similar results.

At Metro Bank stores, we provide standardized, numbered, double-locked safe deposit boxes. Our customers can see exactly where we keep their valuables and they are welcome to come in at any time.

It's another value added and another reason to join Metro Bank.

*

There are four myths of UK retail banking:

- The first is that **no one switches bank accounts**. It must be true because I read it in a London newspaper: people in the UK get divorced more frequently than they switch their accounts. *But it's not true!* Certainly not since July 2010. We're opening up so many new accounts, it's crazy. We surpassed the creation of 100,000 new accounts—and now 700,000+ new accounts—far sooner than we ever dreamed possible.

- The second myth is that **rate is everything**. People *will* come in for great service. They are willing to give up some rate for extraordinary service. Our deposit rates are fair, but our service is our competitive advantage.

- The third is that **a bank can only make money by cutting costs**. Of course not! There are two ways to make money. Grow your top line—that's the best way. Cost cutting is your way to extinction.

- The fourth, of course, is that **the branch is dead**. No way, no how. Not by the volume of in-store traffic that we see. We continually prove that retail customers want the best in every delivery channel and they want the freedom to choose those channels every day. *Our stores are lifelines to our customers.*

When we first opened in Holborn, we had employees of other banks walking in and asking to join us because we threw such a great opening party. Barclays tried to do something to peel off our foot traffic and it was hilarious watching them retaliate. Every day they did something different—and increasingly desperate. First they handed out balloons. The next day they dressed the staff in old-fashioned garb to show how old they were, how old the bank was. I'm sure that enticed people, right? The next day they dressed up the same folk in a more seductive way and had them pole dancing against streetlights. It was crazy! We just watched and laughed. By the end of that week, many of their embarrassed employees crossed the street and inquired about jobs with us.

The conventional wisdom was that nobody could break into the established banking business. The conventional wisdom was that nobody would switch banks. We attacked and disrupted the establishment, earning these incredible results.

*

Customers in New York City were an interesting group. As soon as our retail brand came out, the consumer market responded in a typically New York way: "Now *that's* what I'm talking about! They are open when I need them. They don't charge me fees. They are not rude to me when I walk in. I don't feel like I am crossing into a demilitarized zone. Their physical locations actually look and feel great. Why aren't all banks like this?"

Great models make retailing different, rewarding and fun.

We learned over the years to take nothing for granted. Not the value of a great location and not the value of customers large and small. And we learned it's not just about the *parts* of a model; it's how they fit *together*.

Any successful model needs to be different and create customer value. As Commerce Bank expanded in New York, we had the opportunity to redefine retail banking—and we do again with Metro Bank in Greater London.

And we always try to be a little better tomorrow than we were today. Always.

My View
Howard Flight
Member, House of Lords
Lord Flight is a member of the House of Lords and his wife is

the Lord Mayor of Westminster borough. He has been a non-executive director of Metro Bank since before it opened. He is a traditional Englishman, but he went to the Ross School of Business at the University Michigan in the US. His family—in this case, the Thompsons—made china in the 1800s. Lord Flight has worked for more than 40 years in the financial services industry. He was the Member of Parliament (MP) for Arundel from 1997 to 2005, representing the Tories, before being appointed to the House of Lords by Prime Minister David Cameron in January 2011.

Here is his Metro story, in his own words.

*

It was about 2008, after the sale of Commerce Bank, and Vernon Hill came to London. I and other members of the present board met Vernon through one of the authors of the *Harvard Business Review* study of Commerce.

I liked Vernon immediately because he's such a positive character.

I set up a little bank in the early 1970s, which I then steered through a banking crisis. I wondered whether the style of Metro's proposed branches would be too brash for London, and whether we would gain people's confidence to take their deposits. Otherwise, it was immediately clear that, at Metro, we would offer what people really wanted, which was service. Because the banking cartel in Britain, sort of as a collective decision, gave up providing any service about 20 years ago.

I think there are some Americans who take to Britain, particularly London, like a duck to water, and some that don't. Vernon and Shirley love London. They love meeting all sorts of interesting people, and that comes across. People here like Americans who like our country.

Metro turned up, partly by luck, at absolutely the right time, offering the right service.

Vernon is actually quite a cautious lender. I think that has permeated through the bank, which is a good thing because we had really easy times for the first five years.

Vernon's model is, in essence, what we call an old-fashioned high street bank, with a high level of service and trendy modern trappings.

Metro is a *classic* mom and pop business. I think Shirley does a fantastic job in getting the branches open on time, getting them kitted out. I'm very fond of Shirley because she's a hell of a character, and she's very warm. And I get on with her like a house on fire.

The key success of Metro has been that Craig Donaldson and Vernon get on—and not many people get on as well as they do. Craig has learned a lot from Vernon, and often agrees with him. Vernon knows that he's very lucky to have an extremely good guy running the ship. And he knows when to stand back.

I'm constantly introducing clients to Metro from the House of Lords, and from the other side of the House, too.

They recognize that the banking cartel is not helpful—and that we are. People know that at all levels. A Labor peer told me that his son had built up an interesting business placing good graduates with smaller companies. He needed advice on financing and an account where he would get proper banking service. He tried one of the cartel banks and got a no. I did a bit of phoning on his business to Metro, the account opened speedily, and he has lived happily ever since. I have a lot of these stories. Quite a high proportion of MPs and members of the Lords have Metro Bank accounts now.

6

Love Your Bank At Last!

We only do things that are exciting to us. If it's boring, we walk away.

Daniel Lamarre, president, Cirque du Soleil

"Love Your Bank At Last" is a totally new experience in Britain and it gets to the root of our customer-centric concept.

Consumers value service and convenience. They value walking into a pleasant environment where the doors are open seven days a week. They want multiple channels and multiple access points when dealing with a business partner or a supplier of services, meaning they want it online (**metrobank**online.co.uk), they want to access it on their smartphones, but they also want to be able to talk to somebody live. They want to be able to walk in and see somebody eyeball to eyeball.

Appearance matters, *service* matters, and *convenience* matters.

You can never be too fanatical about service. We have a goal of 100 percent customer service every time, every day, always. While that is physically impossible, it's what we really must strive for, and anything short of that is unacceptable. Once you start setting ratios of 98 percent satisfaction, it's a slippery slope to 96 percent, which is just not acceptable. You can never be too detail oriented. And it is everybody's job to care about everything. Shirley, Craig and I always shop our stores. You have to treat the business like you own it.

Metro Bank is the new and improved version of our American model. Think about it: where else will customers find a bank with extended hours that is open seven days a week? Or where the cashiers don't go to lunch during the customers' lunch hour? We encountered the odd London practice of branch training on Wednesdays, where they close for unannounced lengths of time to train employees about their products. Good for them, but customers don't reliably know when their bank will be open and busy people don't have time to waste waiting around. It will open whenever the bankers finish their training, which might be 10am, or, if training takes a little bit longer, 10.15, *or even later*. It's an insane, insensitive customer policy. It's all about the bankers and what is convenient for them.

A basic flaw in the British banking tradition is that institutions believe that potential customers must *apply* for an account, which is essentially applying to the *bank*. In fact, you have to make an appointment to open a new account.

In our world, to our way of thinking as a depositor, you're lending us your money. What on earth are you applying for? A private club? We should be applying and appealing to *you*.

Let me share with you the story of a pair of young British men who started their own London-based IT business. They had been under "consideration" for an account at one of the traditional high street banks. A decision was ridiculously long in the making. On a whim and out of frustration, they walked into Metro Bank carrying a stack of customer cheques. They could not open an account anywhere else to cash these months-old cheques! We opened their account within an hour and they were thrilled to the point where they said, "If you need us for ads, if you need us for testimonials, if you need us for anything, please ask!" New fans were born.

*

"Love Your Bank At Last" is about having a mission and looking at everything through the eyes of the customer.

We didn't invent banking. What we did was fashion a model that surrounds the customer with convenience, with all the services that everyone else has at fair rates, and with the traditional American banking idea of loving the customer and making everything work for them. The reason people hate the traditional British banks is because they don't have another option.

We tell prospective customers, "Come with us and let's see what a difference we can make in the way you're treated." Where they are accustomed to an unsexy commoditized banking and finance tradition, we present a sexy retail model.

The existing oligarchy used its monopoly power to underinvest in facilities, infrastructure, people, and service. It is saddled with legacy systems, legacy delivery channels, funding problems, capital shortages, and customer disaffection.

We begin with a clean, modern slate designed to create *FANS*.

*

If customers are going to love your business, your marketing must AMAZE them. The *model* is marketing. The *brand* is marketing. *Everything we do* is marketing. I say to new hires, "Everything you do, every day, makes the brand weaker or stronger."

Marketing has the widest possible meaning at Metro Bank, from the red "M" lapel pins to the red "M" cufflinks, from the red "M" door handles to the video displays in our shop windows and everything else we can think of.

At the core of what we do is creating *FANS not customers*. We cannot maintain our growth rate unless our customers are out selling for us all the time, so everything we do reinforces the idea of fans. We are on a mission to redefine our market segment.

There are a number of general precepts under which Metro Bank operates that will translate to almost any smart business. These include:

- the establishment of emotional branding;
- value-added model;
- unified brand delivery;
- best of every delivery channel: in-store, online, mobile, and telephone;
- decentralized delivery, centralized control;
- over-investment in facilities, people and service.

*

One of the greatest points of differentiation between Metro Bank and its competitors—as it was in the US with Commerce Bank—is the emphasis we put on having the best call center in the business. Not in our business but in *any* business.

The people who bank with us never see the Metro Bank customer call center, but it probably influences their opinion of us as much as anything else.

We often had the number one rated American call center at Commerce Bank because we had human beings answering every phone call, *24 hours a day, 7 days a week, 365 days a year*—local people answering the questions and solving the problems of local customers. It became another way to deliver our model instead of just a pain-in-the-butt call center.

And at Metro Bank, we've made delivering customer service better than everyone else in every channel in which customers want access among the highest priorities of our business.

Unlike every other call center, where you have to punch a series of buttons and endure a series of prompts, customers calling Metro Bank get a local person right away who is empowered to take care of them, whatever it takes, around the clock and around the calendar.

Who needs a "Me, Too" call center? Shouldn't we make it another great experience? At Metro Bank, it is.

*

Metro Bank is the ultimate realization of everything I learned at Commerce, reintroduced, and its success in a completely new environment reinforces the concept.

Give the customer legendary service, and one day your company will be a legend, too.

Make your customers happy and they'll become better promoters of your brand, product, and service than the best placed advertisement. Their satisfaction will boost your bottom line like nothing else.

Metro Bank is committed to growth and ours is a growth model. To grow, we must constantly reinvest in people, in processes, in systems, in training, and in facilities. All senior people at the bank are constantly thinking about how to make it better, how to improve it, how to give our customers better service, which makes it a better environment for colleagues as well.

We've built into Metro Bank a cultural safety net to protect our values, best practices, goals, and brand. It's understood across the enterprise that no one is allowed to deviate from the model without talking to my wife, Shirley—the official keeper of the brand—CEO Craig Donaldson, Head of Regional Retail Banking Andrew Richards—who spent over 30 years with us at Commerce Bank—or myself to see if a change makes sense. We always listen for ways that are innovative. But we won't deviate at the expense of the model.

The Keys to Loving Your Bank At Last

- Open 7 days, early and late
- The end of stupid bank rules
- Instant account opening, no appointment necessary
- Instant card and cheque book, printed in store
- Local managers in every store
- Local loans by local lenders
- Great online & mobile banking
- 24/7 local call center, real people with real answers
- Safe deposit boxes, 7-day access
- Instant access savings keeping you on our best rates automatically*

An example of an important change to the model in London was our adoption of e-signature technology in opening new accounts. We no longer generate reams of paper for each new customer—and considering we open 1,000 new accounts daily, that's a huge saving of trees, money and physical storage. When you open an account, we send you a welcome letter by e-mail, rather than by post. This, frankly, is a best practice borrowed from Apple. When you make a purchase at an Apple Store, they say, "Do you want your receipt printed, or do you want us to e-mail it to you?" The light bulb turned on here, and we thought, "Isn't that a cooler way of delivering the service?" We quickly put that into place.

We are always more open to leading edge retail trends rather than following banking trends.

---

* Account opening conditions apply. All Metro Bank products are subject to status and approval.

7

Surprise and Delight!

Simplicity is the ultimate sophistication.

Steve Jobs, co-founder, Apple

We ask our colleagues to treat our business as if they own it and you should ask the same from your employees.

We want them to think. If something doesn't seem right to them, we want them to raise their hand and say, "This doesn't make sense." Or, in answer to an unusual customer request, to say, "You know what? I'm not supposed to do this, but it seems to make sense to me, so let me talk to my supervisor about why I think this should be done." Taking the extra step because it makes sense to do it, even if on an exceptional basis, is okay.

We even have a policy for that: *one to say yes, two to say no.*

In responding to customer requests, our colleagues have two choices: *(1) say "Yes!" and solve the issue on the spot; or (2) find someone else who can.*

Mistakes do happen. That's why we like to acknowledge our errors and demonstrate our ability to recover from them. If we make a mistake, recovering the right way and swiftly will gain that customer's future loyalty. We're a bank that is unafraid of apologizing and we'll even put our money where our apology is with a satisfaction guarantee payment.

Saying "Yes" demands both substance and attitude. We back up the substance behind our attitude by breaking it down in four ways:

- **Product knowledge.** Everyone on the payroll knows Metro's services and products.

- **Company knowledge.** Everyone understands how the company works, and if they can't help, they know someone who can.

- **Listening skills.** We listen, we comprehend, and *then* we respond to the customer.

- **Problem solving skills.** We know how to fix things, and we know how to fix them fast.

We design guidelines that outline procedures and policies for operating our business as efficiently as possible. Inevitably, they occasionally interfere with providing excellent customer service. That's why, whenever a customer's need conflicts with an established policy or procedure, we tell our Metro Bank colleagues to use their best judgment and/or "bump it up" to a supervisor.

"No" is not the only word that creates immediate negative images. Over the years, we identified forbidden phrases to avoid, the kind that can drive customers crazy in needless frustration or anger.

Here are our suggested alternatives:

Forbidden phrase	Use instead
"We can't do that"	"Let me get some help to resolve this." "Is there someone (or something) else we can do?"
"I don't know"	"I'll find out." Customers expect us to know something!
"Sorry you'll have to …"	"Here's how we can help you with that…" We're servicing the customer; the customer shouldn't have to do anything.

We strive every day to avoid inconveniencing our customers. Saying "Yes" means maintaining a "can do" approach.

Fans are created by great companies committed to resolving inevitable problems with a positive approach.

*

Our fans feel loved and respected when they arrive at Metro Bank and are greeted—every day. Some days are easier than other days, naturally.

- Just before closing one Sunday, our Staines store received a call from a distressed customer. He explained that he'd just returned from Devon and could not find his bank card. As he had a cash account, he was unable to make online transfers, and was stranded with no access to his money. Metro colleague Shamilah Mughal surprised and delighted the customer by telling him the store would stay open so that he could come and collect his new card. The customer was amazed that Metro would go so far above and beyond his expectations and stay past closing time to accommodate him.

- The Earl's Court store received a phone call from an anxious customer. He told our customer service representative, Mark Nsianguana, that he'd lost his card and cheque book and wouldn't be able to visit the store straight away, as he was going to be in the hospital for a few weeks. Nsianguana visited the customer in the hospital to personally deliver a brand new card and cheque book.

- An elderly woman visited the Holborn store to make a cash deposit. Cashier Adil Nunchuck not only provided fantastic service but then escorted her across busy streets so she could get to the train station safely. While this happened, a passer-by witnessed this kindness and sent an e-mail to the store about it. The message said, "I just wanted to drop a note to truly praise the staff at your Holborn branch. I witnessed Adil escorting/assisting an older lady through the hustle and bustle that is High Holborn, to the safety of the tube station. This is an act of kindness that you rarely witness, especially in the banking sector. I was bowled over, truly, and for that reason, I am currently reviewing your products with a view to moving."

- A customer visiting the Metro Bank store in Windsor made his way to the teller line to deposit funds he converted from loose change in the Magic Money Machine into his account. Assistant store manager Asher John noticed something sparkling inside the machine. He removed the cover and, upon closer inspection, found a bracelet. Asher quickly called the customer over and showed him what he'd found. The customer became emotional, overwhelmed by Asher's quick thinking. He explained that the bracelet was a gift from his late wife and that he'd been looking for it since she passed away.

Every day at Metro Bank, there are colleagues undertaking similarly Good Samaritan tasks in the name of service and building fans!

*

The Metro store in Slough opened in 2013 and was one of the first in a series of suburban locations that will bring drive-thru banking to the United Kingdom. It's a feature taken for granted in the United States, but relatively new here.

We had to teach both our Metro Bank colleagues and the first wave of Slough customers how to use it, which was fun. Growing up in the US, drive-thru banking is one of those things that you absorb from childhood: "This is a drive-thru; this is what you do."

For the first few weeks of operation, we stationed colleagues in the drive-thru. As new customers arrived and wanted to try it for the first time, they would walk them through the drawer, explain which button to push, and how the pneumatic tube pulled and pushed their transaction papers back and forth to the teller inside the store.

Drive-thru banking was an instant hit, both with parents traveling with children and everyone else who didn't have to leave the comfort of their warm, dry automobiles on a cold, wet day, providing another choice—another customer convenience.

*

Your customers arrive at your door each day with an array of emotions and needs to be satisfied.

What follows are examples of the ways our colleagues make them all feel special. Your team can do this too, no matter what business you are in:

- Smile.
- Immediately give their undivided attention.
- Speak in a friendly tone of voice.
- Address external customers by name.
- Express a sincere desire to help.
- Say "Thank you!"

Good verbal communication is at the core of customer service. Spoken (and written) words are only a small portion of customer perception.

What do we do with non-verbal communication to make the customer feel special?

Here are our top tips:

- **Stand.** By being ready on our feet, we demonstrate an eagerness to help.

- **Eye contact.** Looking customers in the eye lets them know we recognize them as individuals.

- **Silence.** At times, we communicate without saying a word. Listening while customers speak is a sign of respect; nodding lets them know we hear them. (Prolonged silence, however, can leave customers dubious. An occasional verbal acknowledgement shows that we're still listening, without interrupting.)

- **Gestures.** Open gestures welcome customers; crossed arms, hands tucked deep in pockets, or clenched fists create non-verbal barriers. Open gestures welcome customers into our offices and stores.

- **Posture.** Mother said "stand up straight" for good reason. Good posture demonstrates competence and confidence.

- **Overall appearance.** Being neat and clean sends a basic message of competence.

- **Facial expression.** A raised eyebrow indicates surprise; a wink conveys agreement or connection; tightly set lips mean "No"; a big smile implies friendliness.

These are further opportunities to convert customers into fans.

*

Customers can *always* expect us to keep our promises. And once they know they can expect this, we are in a position to shape expectations to match what we can do for them.

Responsive and immediate action is more critical to success and creating fans than ever before. More and more businesses sell themselves on their commitment to getting things done quickly:

- Federal Express—"Absolutely, Positively, Overnight"

building the brand

FANS!
NOT CUSTOMERS

legendary brands
(experiences)

emotional brands
(feelings)

basic brands
(brand promise)

---

chiefs in the 20-20-20 club — Forbes.com

Members of the Forbes 20-20-20 Club are chief executives who've held the top job for 20 years at a company with publicly traded shares for at least 20 years, who have presided over at least 20% annual return since the company went public.

Chief Executive Officer	Company	Tenure as Chief (years)	Annualized Total Return During Tenure	Annualized Total Return Relative to S&P 500
Lawrence J. Ellison	Oracle	30	31%	117
Howard Solomon	Forest Labs	30	29%	115
Warren E. Buffett	Berkshire Hathaway	37	27%	114
Vernon W. Hill II	**Commerce Bancorp**	**34**	**23%**	**109**
Harold M. Messmer Jr.	Robert Half Int'l.	21	23%	110
Alan I. Kirshner	Markel	21	22%	109
Leslie H. Wexner	Limited Brands	44	21%	106

Source: Forbes.com, May 2007 - Andrea D. Murphy

On September 26, 1996, Commerce Bancorp began trading on the New York Stock Exchange und the symbol CBH, becoming "America's Most Convenient Bank." Five years later, in January 2002, Commerce was invited back to the NYSE to ring the bell again.

Six thousand Commerce Bank team members attended the 2005 Wow Awards at the legendary Radio City Music Hall in New York City.

wife, Shirley, and I greeted prospective customers at the grand opening of the first Metro Bank in born, London. Shirley is holding our Yorkshire terrier, Duffy, who welcomed their dogs.

Britain's top rated morning show, BBC's *Breakfast*, broadcasts live at the Holborn Grand Opening.

Reading

Design is a competitive weapon at Metro Bank. Our stores reflect the brand, with open, inviting, and fun interiors.

Romford

Metro Bank makes banking fun. Magic Money Machines, the coin counting devices in every Metro Bank lobby, are free to use and great fun. If you want to guess the value of your coins with our interactive game–you could even win a prize!

We've even had dogs using them–dogs rule at Metro Bank.

On October 23, 2015 we opened London's first drive-thru bank in the heart of Southall.

ATTEND *to every detail*

MAKE *every wrong, right*

ASK *if you're not sure–*
Bump it up!

ZEST *is contagious–*
Share it!

EXCEED *expectations*

We believe there are five ways to AMAZE every Metro Bank customer.

March 26, 2016, Metro Bank begins trading on the London Stock Exchange as "MTRO."

Each year we hold an awards ceremony to celebrate our amazing culture.

METRO BANK

PROMISE

- ☑ **surprise & delight** every customer

- ☑ **deliver unlimited convenience**
  - 📍 in-store
  - 🖥 online
  - 📞 mobile
  - 📱 phone

- ☑ **no stupid bank rules**

- ☑ **satisfaction guaranteed**

- Pizza Hut—"5-Minute Meal Guarantee" (at lunchtime)
- Lens Crafters—"Custom-crafted eyeglasses in about an hour"

We set and *meet* deadlines. That's important. Deadlines are *created*. If we say, "We'll have it for you this afternoon," or "We'll mail it today," we create an expectation and set a deadline for ourselves. Be realistic! Because once created, deadlines are the measure by which customers will define your success or failure.

Create acceptable, realistic expectations of responsiveness for customers and meet those expectations.

*

What we did at Metro Bank was to transport the American concept of community banking: we're here to service the customer.

In community banking, one person is the customer's banker. The same person handles the relationship and the customer deals with that team member almost exclusively.

The British model—and, frankly, the US model at many large banks—is totally different. One person develops the business and hands it over to a second person, who underwrites it and makes the loan decision and hands it over to a third person, who handles the account going forward. It's called the "Finder, Grinder, Minder" model.

A real banker wants to handle the entire relationship. That's something the industry did successfully 30 years ago, but the banking model in both the US and the UK has slipped away from it.

*

Metro Bank doesn't put 25 hurdles between itself and its

customers, forestalling a loan decision. The people they need to see to make a loan decision are on the premises every day.

We are local lenders making local loans.

We empower our Metro Bank colleagues as entrepreneurs, just as we did at Commerce Bank. By our definition, an entrepreneur has an ownership interest in the business. We convert our colleagues into entrepreneurs by sharing an ownership interest in the bank, not only because they might have bought stock, but also because they are incentivized through stock options. Stock options give colleagues the right to buy shares in the company at a fixed price, which means that as the market value of the company goes up, so does the value of their stock.

The wealth creation at Commerce was a product of stock options and it motivated our colleagues monetarily, literally staking them to an ownership interest. All Metro Bank employees receive stock options, which—if the bank performs as we anticipate it will—a number of years down the road will create a lot of new wealth.

Options create a unique relationship. The number of options awarded is based on an individual's performance. The value of the options is determined by the performance of the entire bank.

Metro Bank employees take a personal pride in their colleagueship that you won't see at other banks. At other banks, there's really no pride in going to work each day. It's just a job.

Join Metro Bank and you're part of a model that is revolutionizing British banking. It's a service model where people come to work and enjoy themselves, which is why it is becoming more and more common to see Metro Bank team member pins being worn all over London. Customers recognize the big red "M" and smile at the wearer. They say, "Wow! You work for my bank, and you're obviously as proud of the affiliation as I am!"

It's just one more way we convert customers into *FANS*.

8

Dogs Rule and Kids Rock!

> Histories are more full of examples of the fidelity of dogs than of friends.
>
> Alexander Pope, 18th century poet, *The Rape of the Lock*

At Metro Bank, we throw out the welcome mat to our customers' dogs.

Some people might think our "Love Your Bank At Last" slogan is aimed at dogs. And we won't deny that.

We welcome your dog into our stores. Dogs have become members of the family—you wouldn't chain your children to the tree outside and leave them there, would you? We've got fresh water in the front entrance waiting for them. We'll give them free treats and a cool Metro Bank bandana to wear.

Why? *Because if we love your dog, you know we love you, too.*

Our initiatives are about being all the things that will make anyone feel like a loved and valued member of the Metro Bank community. We're the people who sponsor the local football team and we're there at all the times when you need us most.

On opening day at Holborn, the only people who brought their dogs in were the ones we personally invited. We were right there at the front door, Shirley and I, with our own pup, Sir Duffield, "Duffy" for short. Londoners had to see it to believe such behavior would be truly acceptable, no matter what they read in our ads and marketing literature.

We have dogs in the stores all the time, an emotional branding twist that is entirely due to Shirley's influence.

The story starts with what is now an embarrassing truth: I would never let our four children have a dog or a cat. I always thought of pets in terms of negatives: messy, noisy, disruptive, unpredictable. We had a rabbit for a month—only because Shirley and the kids hid him in the laundry room.

But when the last of our four children went off to college, Shirley informed me she had waited long enough.

"I'm getting a dog," she said.

"No, you're not," I said.

Growing up, I never had a dog. I didn't *want* a dog. I barely spoke to Shirley for two or three days. I was *really* anti-dog.

Two days after she made the announcement, I said, "You're not really doing this, are you?"

"Yes, I am," she said. "We're going to get a Yorkshire terrier."

She and our daughter drove for several hours to a Yorkie breeder that they had vetted. They were gone a long time so I called and said, "Where are you? Are you okay?"

"We're fine," she said. "There are two dogs and this other couple was here before us. We're waiting for them to decide which dog they want."

It took the other family four long hours, but Shirley ultimately got the one she wanted. And as the dogs were only eight weeks old, the girls had to wait five more weeks until they were weaned. During that time, I tried again to shake their determination to bring a dog into our lives.

"Vernon," Shirley said, "we're going to have to get an auto carrier for the dog when we go in the summer to the beach house every weekend."

"No dog is getting in my car, Shirley," I told her. "We don't need any carriers because there will be no dog going with us."

Let me cut to the chase: she got the dog.

Our friends and associates, knowing my longstanding aversion to household pets, placed bets on how long it would be before the dog would be sleeping in our bed. I told them they were crazy to even suggest such a thing.

It took three days.

Events—and Duffy himself—overcame my wariness of being a dog owner. Even as I was coming to love the dog on his terms, I joined the board of the University of Pennsylvania and then the Board of the School of Veterinary Medicine.

Duffy became a differentiator for the Hill family, for Commerce Bank, and now for Metro Bank.

The Brits love their dogs and Duffy became very, very big news in London. He also became an icebreaker for me, because whenever I have Duffy, people can't help themselves; everyone wants to meet him. (If I'd known that when I was in high school, I would have had one then. The dog is a chick magnet!)

As for Metro Bank's policy of not only allowing but encouraging dogs in our stores, it goes back to 2001 when we were preparing to open the first Commerce Bank stores in New York City and Shirley was in the city, shopping our soon-to-be competition, experiencing the practices of different banks. Duffy was with her at every stop.

At most banks, the guard would stop them at the front entrance. "I'm sorry," they would say. "No dogs allowed in here."

If she made it inside, somebody else would come rushing up and say the same thing.

Shirley, fed up, finally went outside and called me.

"Do me a favor," she said, "please check the state and federal bank regulations and find out if there is something on the books that says that a dog cannot go inside a bank."

Three days later, I reported back. "We can't find anything," he said.

At that moment, "Dogs Rule!" was born.

*

Duffy has his own Twitter feed: @SirDuffield. He tweets every day to his mates and has attracted more than 3,000 followers. People tweet earnestly in response to his posts. The whole "Dogs Rule" campaign was a success in New York, but it's way wilder in Britain. I often get stopped on the streets of London and people say, "Aren't you the banker with the dog?"

The little guy is a columnist for *Revolution News*, the bank's official newsletter. It's called "Duffy's Dish." He shares photos of his friends and always has something to say about new dogs that have been seen in the bank. Our colleagues even carry Duffy business cards. When they talk to someone about a loan and they show a picture of their dog and their children, it's a great, great icebreaker; their hearts melt.

Every year since Metro Bank opened its doors and welcomed our first customers and their dogs, we've earned the "Open for Dogs on the High Street" award from the Kennel Club. It has an ongoing campaign to open up more businesses and public places in the city to dogs. Five years and five awards later, the other banks still ban dogs. They just don't know how easy it is and how much it improves the lives of everyone they meet.

I'm the perfect example of that. We live it; if Duffy won't be welcome somewhere, we won't go there, either.

*

Sadly, the original Duffy died suddenly in 2015 at the age of 12.

We were traveling back to the United States from London when Duffy collapsed. Doctors from the University of Pennsylvania Vet school met the plane when we landed and tried desperately to save the little guy; his lungs were full of fluid, making his breathing labored and increasingly difficult. Shirley called Duffy's breeder, Cindy Hill, to see if she had any experience with this situation and advice to offer. Unfortunately, she did not.

The doctors did everything they could but, ultimately, it was just Duffy's time and we had to say goodbye.

It was one of the saddest days our family could remember.

Shirley talked to the breeder again soon after. By a remarkable coincidence, she had three puppies on hand that were direct descendants of the dame and sire that produced Duffy. Unfortunately, all three were already promised to families.

A day later, Cindy called back.

"Shirley," she said, "I've been thinking about this. Duffy's father is the grandfather of this litter, of these three dogs. And a woman who was going to take one of these dogs hasn't sent her cheque. It was due last week. Also, this dog is going directly to a trainer. He'll never have a normal life. He'll be on a show circuit for much of his life."

Shirley listened, wondering where the conversation would lead.

"This dog is yours. He has to be yours. Duffy willed this dog to be yours."

Shirley and I flew to Virginia the next day and adopted Duffy II. (His grandfather was Duffy I's father.)

Once the pup was in our hands, I called Craig Donaldson and told him everything that had happened.

"This is big," Craig said. "Duffy is an integral part of the Metro brand. We have to celebrate the original Duffy. And we have to welcome the new one."

*

Everyone asks how is Duffy II different from Duffy I?

This one is smarter. How do I know this? Because the dog likes *me* more, of course!

The first Duffy was totally Shirley's dog. This time, I was

immediately on board with getting a new dog. "We're going to get this dog," I said. I picked him up. We bonded instantly.

The first dog, his body was a temple. He was a little aloof. He wouldn't jump off things; he waited to be picked up. He was a very particular dog. This one is fearless. The first puppy was Prince William; this is Prince Harry. When we tell the Brits that, they get it. This one has a unique personality. He's also more approachable and more personable. He loves grand openings. The first one hated thunder and lightning, and would howl at it. This one isn't afraid. This one likes Metro Man; the first Duffy didn't care for Metro Man too much. This Duffy is *definitely* Chief Canine Officer.

*

In the UK, we're the official bank for the Kennel Club and we do weekend doggie adopt-a-thons with Battersea Dogs & Cats Home, which is world famous and is supported by the Royal Family.

The Kennel Club is the largest organization in the UK devoted to dog health, welfare and training. Its objective is to ensure that dogs live healthy, happy lives with responsible owners.

It invests in welfare campaigns, dog training, education programs, and the Kennel Club Charitable Trust, which supports research into dog diseases and dog welfare charities, including Kennel Club Breed Rescue organizations that rehome dogs throughout the UK.

We are extremely pleased to be their official banking partner and to play our part in their Open for Dogs campaign. Metro Bank is all about convenience, and that is what we offer. You should not be forced to leave your dog outside banks that are supposed to be serving you. We're here to do things differently from other London high street banks.

Rosemary Smart, the Kennel Club's chief executive, said: "It is refreshing to see a new breed of bank, which recognizes that dogs are part of the family and incorporates that into its business policy."

Metro Bank has won an award in the Kennel Club's prestigious Open for Dogs Competition three years running. We were nominated by the public in the annual competition's London high street category, beating other well-known high street businesses to scoop this top award.

The Kennel Club's Open for Dogs campaign aims to break down barriers for man's best friend by encouraging more businesses to be dog-friendly. This is supported by research released by the Kennel Club which shows that a staggering four out of five businesses claim that their dog-friendly policy has helped them draw in more customers in difficult financial times.

Metro Bank's appreciation of its canine-loving customers paid off, as dozens of nominations flooded in to support the bank each day, helping us to beat the stiff competition. One member of the public who nominated Metro Bank commented on its "refreshing way of doing business," which helped to secure nominations.

Caroline Kisko, communications director at the Kennel Club, said:

> The winners of these awards are determined by the public, who recognize that Metro Bank is willing to go above and beyond for its customers and that dog-friendly businesses are an important part of the British high street. Metro Bank is a fine example of the many companies and organizations that are reaping the benefits of a dog-friendly door policy in terms of creating a welcome atmosphere, as well as helping to secure itself financially by widening its customer base.

The Kennel Club has found that 95 percent of people think more businesses and locations should be open for dogs, and that dogs improve the atmosphere of a place, and 77 percent think that dogs help to reduce stress.

*

Great brands become great community members. That's part of the reason Metro Bank UK also has a children's banking initiative called "Kids Rock."

It starts with a "5 for 5 Club" in which children under 11 open a savings account with us. We encourage them to return and make deposits of their own by providing a special club membership card and a plastic "M" money box to store coins in between visits. Each time they return, the kids get a prize and the card is punched. When they have five punches, we put £5 in the account to celebrate. We want their trip to Metro Bank to be as anticipated and thrilling as a visit to McDonald's.

At 11, a youngster can have a Metro Bank savings account in their own name, which is an exciting day in many children's lives.

The "Metro Money Zone" educational program teaches kids about money, finance, savings, and the importance of making and sticking to a budget. We put together a sophisticated, accredited program in which we go into year 4 and year 5 classrooms for three sessions. The fourth session is held on site at the neighborhood Metro Bank.

We're passionate about what we do, so we believe we're well placed to spread that passion by sharing our knowledge of all things financial. Our Money Zone program works with schools in the community, giving children an understanding of the basic principles of money, saving, and banking in an engaging and fun way (and in line with the National Curriculum). The highlight is when the kids visit our stores, open their accounts, meet Metro Man, and become new fans.

Kids Rock at Metro Bank, which in simple terms means we

value our younger customers and believe that banking should be made fun. Aside from the friendly and welcoming experience you'll get from visiting your local store, there's an array of fun stuff to enjoy: win prizes using our Magic Money Machine, enjoy free lollipops, save your coins in our M Banks, and much more. There are just so many reasons to visit!

Great brands become great community members.

Part 3

Fanatical Execution

9

Eight Ways to Be AMAZE(ING)

Be a yardstick of quality. Some people aren't used to an environment where excellence is expected.

Steve Jobs, co-founder, Apple

To create a great business, create a pervasive culture that executes a differentiated model. And fanatically execute to exceed expectations.

Our goal is to revolutionize British banking by creating *FANS not customers*. And the number one customer principle that will take us there can be summarized in one word: AMAZEing!

Our job is to execute the model and reinforce the model, and—whenever possible—improve the model. Culture is the way people behave. It's how we do things around here. Culture is the model in action. Lots of organizations will have a vision, values, and behaviors.

You can't see someone's values, but we can see how they behave and infer what their values are from that behavior.

We ask colleagues to attend to every detail, and to make every one right, and to ask a second person if they're not sure about telling a customer "No."

Our values and our behaviors are the *same* thing. The *value* is that we want to attend to every detail. And the *behavior* is that we attend to every detail.

Here's how we spell it out and explain it consistently to Metro Bank colleagues.

A—Attend to Every Detail

Retail is in the detail, so make sure that your store always looks its best. Keep your facilities in pristine condition for customers to enjoy and appreciate. Are your marketing materials current?

Make sure that you attend to every detail of the customer experience, and that whatever issue you're dealing with is accurate. All it takes to scare off a new customer is misspelling their name once.

Here are some examples of how Metro Bank colleagues have attended to every detail:

- A customer came to Bromley to transfer his ISA and open a £50,000 fixed bond with Metro Bank. While waiting for credit references to approve and backdate the £50,000 bond, a customer service representative offered him a cup of coffee, then thought, "Why not offer him some biscuits, too?" Because he extended this simple courtesy, the customer cancelled putting the year's allowance into a Nationwide variable ISA and instead took out another ISA with us.

- A Metro Bank colleague had a customer who only spoke Arabic. Unable to find another colleague who could translate, he called several friends until he found one who could translate for him. He put the customer on the phone and was able to complete the desired transaction. The customer was AMAZEd and deposited £35,000 into a new account.

- A Metro Bank colleague set up a loan for a customer who requested that the funds be dispersed in two weeks. In the meantime, the loan rate was dramatically reduced, from 10 percent to 7.9 percent. Realizing that this meant the customer was not getting the best possible deal, the assistant store manager told the team member to invite the customer back to the store so that he could receive the new rate—a saving of more than £420. The customer felt the team member had exceeded his expectations and returned to the store a third time to present her with a box of chocolates and a bottle of wine.

M—Make Every Wrong, Right

To err is human and to recover is divine. So, if we *do* make a mistake—because we are human—we want to make sure that we apologize to our customer and also that we give them what we call a satisfaction guarantee. We put our money where our mouth is and if we make a mistake, we give customers money for it. *Apologize! Fix it right away!* And make sure that their satisfaction is guaranteed every time.

- When we had a processing problem with MasterCard, it came to our attention that a customer couldn't pay for their airline flights. A Metro Bank colleague stepped in. She put the customer's flights on her *personal* credit card so that the customer could still take advantage of a good deal, and transferred the money—with permission, of course—from their account.

- One evening at 9pm, our IT system crashed and the call center was unable to access customer accounts or details. At that time, a customer called to transfer funds from his ISA to his current account. He explained that it was extremely urgent as he needed to pay a bill in the morning before leaving for work. A Metro Bank colleague promised the customer that the payment would be made and said he would call him back as soon as the issue was resolved and the payment completed. An hour later, he called the customer to explain that the problem had not yet been resolved, but he would stay in the office until the system was back up. It was finally fixed at 11.10pm. He contacted the customer the following morning to make sure he was able to withdraw his funds. The customer made a point of telling us how impressed he was that the Metro Bank colleague had stayed on the job to see through the urgent transaction.

A—Ask If You're Not Sure, Bump It Up

At Metro Bank, it takes just one person to say "Yes" to a customer but *two* to say "No." So, if somebody has a request that a cashier or customer service representative or loan officer is not sure they can approve, we do not automatically say "No." We "bump it up" to a supervisor. Then the supervisor and the colleague come to a conclusion together. We empower our employees; if they feel that it's the right thing to do, they have the authority within certain guidelines to make decisions on behalf of the customer's welfare and benefit. But if they're not sure, they *ask*. Bump it up. Never say no at the first opportunity. Look for an alternative solution that leads to a "Yes!"

- At a training course a colleague asked why self-authorization for a customer was capped at £5,000, when an ISA allowance is £5,000. This rule caused extra permissions to be sought every time. By bumping this up to our chief executive, who immediately changed the threshold, customers and colleagues have been saved a great deal of time and frustration.

- A customer was due to leave for holiday at midday on a Friday and he had not received a promised new debit card in the post. A Metro Bank colleague spoke to both the Borehamwood store and the customer to try to remedy the situation. Unfortunately, the customer was busy at work and could not travel to another store to pick up a replacement. The colleague bumped it up, printed the card at the Holborn store, arranged for a new PIN, and personally delivered the card to the customer at home that night.

Z—Zest is Contagious, Share It

Zest is all about behaviors. When you come in to work during the day, we want you to have a zest for your job that shows. We want you to be happy. We want your customer to see that you're happy. We want you to share that zest with everyone around you so the customer feels it from the second that they walk in, through their entire transaction and until the time that they leave. That's what makes us different.

- A customer service representative collapsed during training and the paramedics were called. While she was in the ambulance, she told them about how good Metro Bank was and sent a colleague back to the store to make up goody bags for the paramedics who had helped her. At a later date, they all came back to the Kensington High Street store for a visit—and all opened accounts!

E—Exceed Expectations

Exceed the *customer's* expectations. If a customer comes in and makes a deposit, instead of just giving them a receipt and saying, "Thank you very much," ask, "Is there anything else that I can do for you? Would you like the balance on your account?" Go the extra meter.

- An Uxbridge colleague noticed that a customer was about to go out in the rain in a lovely suit. She asked him if he'd like an umbrella and gave him her own to ensure he didn't get wet. He came back the next day to return the umbrella and deposited £10,000. But that wasn't the end of the story; he brought along several family members who all opened new accounts.

- Another customer came in to our Uxbridge store and explained that she'd been the victim of fraud: her account had been cleared. She had no cash on her and was worried about how she was going to pay for food for her family over the coming weekend. While several colleagues helped untangle her account and restore its balance, others bought the customer several bags of food to ensure that her family did not go hungry.

- Croydon colleagues helped a customer whose handbag was stolen the day before she was due to leave on holiday. Staff kept the store open until the customer was able to get there at 8.45pm. They printed her a new card and ordered in food to share with the happy customer. They then walked her to her car and even paid her parking fee.

*

Three years into Metro Bank's existence, Danielle "Danny" Harmer shared an observation with Craig Donaldson.

"I think AMAZE is great for teaching colleagues what Metro Bank is all about and how to execute our vision," she said, "But there are no leadership values in there. We need to expand our approach so that the message inspires executives and managers as well."

"Fine," Craig said. "But we're not changing AMAZE."

(Craig had famously devised and defined AMAZE on the back of a beer napkin in a London pub in the days leading up to the first Metro Bank store opening.)

"You can have -ing—I, N, G," he said. "AMAZE-ING. Come up with something, and we'll add it on."

That's what she did. New to this second edition of *FANS Not Customers* are the following additions to our famous formula that took us from AMAZE to AMAZE(ING).

I—Inspire Colleagues to Create Fans

- Set and communicate clear objectives so people know what they need to achieve.
- Inspire colleagues to be at their best for themselves and the organization.
- Make decisions with the information available.
- Be honest and open, you can rely on me.
- Hold yourself and your team accountable.
- Share AMAZE(ING) stories which bring to life the Metro mission for our people.

N—Nurture Colleagues so they Grow

- Select and develop talented people who are a great cultural fit.
- Create helpful networks and connections within Metro Bank.
- Look for ways to improve the way you lead our people.
- Understand the perspectives of others.
- Take responsibility.
- Set aside time to mentor team members.

G—Game Change

- Always improve.
- Understand and stay connected to our customers and colleagues and the environment in which we operate.
- Understand our people challenges and our commercial risks.

- Make things simple for our customers and colleagues and fix any issues.

*

Successful, customer-facing businesses try to see things from the customer's point of view. Stand in the customer's shoes. Don't hide behind rules; don't hide behind policies.

Think about going out to dinner at a restaurant:

- Before you enter a restaurant, you evaluate it based on the location, the advertising and the look of the people who work there. Is the car park clean? Can you smell the aroma of good food or the remains of half-eaten meals in the dustbin?
- As you walk through the door, you make more judgments. Do the employees look friendly? Are you greeted at the door and made to feel welcome?
- During the meal you evaluate the items on the menu from how well the food is presented to how it tastes.
- Most importantly, how well are you being served? Kindly? Or with utter disinterest and contempt?

The best rule of thumb is never do or give something to a customer you would be embarrassed, reluctant, or angered to receive yourself.

*

What the public doesn't see inside our businesses is that we take the excellent customer service shown to external clients and apply its precepts internally as well.

- During the Christmas holidays, customers have brought in biscuits and presents for the staff because they had been treated so well.

voted #1
for customer service

2 NOVEMBER 2014

THE SUNDAY TIMES

MONEY MADE EASY
YOUR FIVE-MINUTE GUIDE TO...
BANK CUSTOMER SERVICE

The established high street banks have some of the worst customer
satisfaction ratings, with building societies and new "challenger" banks
topping the tables instead.

A new survey, conducted by the consumer group Fairer Finance, has highlighted
how some of the big names are failing their customers, driving growing numbers
of them to vote with their feet.

The top overall score went to Metro bank with 93%.

METRO BANK	**93%**
First Direct	83%
Halifax	63%
TSB	54%
Lloyds Bank	35%
Barclays	30%
Santander	25%
Royal Bank of Scotland	6%

- We celebrate when an employee has shown extra initiative to discover a "customer" trying to commit fraud and catching it before anything bad happened.

- Metro Maniacs will visit stores and create a big fuss around team members that provided extraordinary service.

There are two primary Metro Bank Twitter accounts. The first is @Metro_Bank, which is used for several bank purposes. The second, @MetroBank_Help, is being used as a help channel, where people come for assistance and receive official responses from AMAZE Direct, which is our 24/7 call center. It allows us to speed up responses to customers who choose to contact us via Twitter rather than telephone. The benefit is that our customer service representatives have immediate access to all the systems (and managers) and can promptly assist customers with any query.

Another way we recognize top service internally is a circle

of excellence dinner called "The AMAZE Awards." People are nominated for recognition and our leadership team evaluates their success stories and then everybody votes. There is participation throughout all levels of the Metro Bank organization. All the nominees are invited and the winners are celebrated at a Metro Bank awards event.

Our colleagues are rewarded for amazing customers and creating *FANS*.

10

Culture Counts!

**Passion and standing up for things can help create a sense
of unity. But you still have to act a certain way.**

Arthur Blank, co-founder, The Home Depot

We have created a culture to match our model.

Anyone who has done business at or with Metro Bank—or
joined the team—knows that we are different.

Culture—and recognition—was so important at Commerce that we had annual "WOW! Awards" to recognize our
top-performing stores, reinforce our culture and reward our
outstanding achievers—over 8,000 of them each year. We didn't
just put on a party hat to celebrate our success, we rented the
legendary Radio City Music Hall, and put on a gala show which
included everything from a Commerce Bank team member
talent show to the world famous Rockettes themselves.

Of course we do not do everything right. There will always
be bumps in the road. But we keep and maintain our competitive advantage because we're not at the end; we have a long way
to go.

I am often asked, "How can Metro Bank sustain its
culture?" I consistently respond, "Metro has never been about

maintenance." Every day we seek to *improve* the culture, to rise to a higher level. We want to move the ball further down the field.

If you have a culture that wants to create fans and wants to have no stupid rules and wants to exceed customer expectations, *you will succeed*. But if you've got a culture driven only by making money, with a focus on getting costs down and driving productivity up, *you will not*.

You can try to cost-cut your way to prosperity, or you can grow your way to prosperity—obviously, we believe in the latter. Growth companies believe in their growth model and they invest and over-invest to grow their model and they create value through growth. Companies that do not have a growth model and try to cost-cut their way to prosperity rarely, if ever, succeed. At Metro Bank, for example, we overspend on buildings, on locations; we're open seven days, which is more expensive than weekday-only banking; and we make a substantial investment in the design and training for AMAZE Direct, our call centers—although no customer will ever set foot there. We consistently over-invest for returns where our competition under-invests.

Many banks in the UK want to drive costs down, drive productivity up, and deliver modest customer service—but in *that* order.

What we want to create are fans, amazing service and convenience, and that is what we do. If you're trying to achieve great culture, great service, great convenience and to attract customers who will introduce other people to you, that's the basis for your decisions. If that's the core of everything you do, that's what you achieve. People look for a single silver bullet, but it's the million things you put together, and at the center of the million things is the culture.

Ultimately, the culture of Metro Bank is centered on our colleagues and the often heroic things that our people do that delight our customers with service. That's another way we generate *FANS not customers*. We want to AMAZE them with service every day and always.

In 2013, we began using a Microsoft application called Yammer, internally, to allow everyone in the bank to share stories of our colleagues' good deeds and heroic outreach.

Basically, it's a business-oriented Facebook, and there was some initial nervousness around turning it on. We said, "Let's just turn it on and see what happens. And if it's an issue, we'll turn it off."

Some people used it quite oddly. But Yammer had great power when people started sharing—quite a lot of our employees are young, as you might expect—photos and stories about great customer and colleague experiences. They latched on to Yammer to share remarkable, often heart-warming stories that reinforce our culture.

The other thing that we saw people using it for was virtual bump-ups. If you have a process or culture question and don't know whom to phone, you can post a question to the entire organization in a flash or tag a particular team for their attention. By adding a tag, they'll get an email saying, "Craig tagged you in a question, you better go and answer it."

There's an "attaboy" praise option in Yammer as well, so colleagues use it to praise each other, generally in connection to a customer service experience.

An American company called Recognize created a plugin that works in conjunction with Yammer. Shirley's company, InterArch, created a virtual badge for each of our AMAZE-ing behaviors. For example, we have one for "attend to every detail" and another for "make every one right." If I think a Metro Bank colleague has done something that suggests they attended to every detail, I can award them a badge and it appears in the internal Yammer feed. You are recognized for behaving in relation to our culture. If fellow colleagues like the story and think it worthy of a badge, they can award an extra point. And if they don't, it disappears to the bottom. It's a peer-to-peer, anyone-to-anyone recognition approach.

Once a month we organize a surprise and delight event, where we invite people who've had the best stories or the most badges. We've had ice-skating at Somerset House, ten-pin bowling, two rotations around the London Eye with champagne, pasta cooking lessons, and cake decorating with a BBC "MasterChef" winner.

Occasionally people might post social photographs on Yammer, as long as the pictures are sensible and work-related. But it doesn't happen often. A great example was a photo from the IT Department's 2014 IT Christmas party in which there was a photo of the guys dancing. It was probably one of the most popular Yammer posts of the year, because everyone knew those guys. Day in and day out, they're always so serious. But here they were, letting their hair down and having a dance. The entire team saw these hard-working men and women in a refreshing new light.

If there is an issue in the business such as fraud in one of the stores, we can mobilize support quickly and share whatever information we have with every store to protect the bank. Yammer gets the word out even faster than email in many cases.

*

The typical bank model is:

- High cost of deposits
- Low operating costs
- Low growth

  Our model is:

- Lower cost of deposit

- High service delivery costs
- High growth

We acquire customers with service and convenience, not price.

British banks are run as utilities with no brand loyalty to their customers. Do you know anyone in love with their no- or low-competition utility companies? Doubtful. Few people love BT (British Telecom). Isn't there something terribly wrong when your telephone provider doesn't answer your call?

The British banking cartel manages from the expense side: for them, growth, if any, comes via acquisition.

We are *completely* different.

The pillars of our disruptor model include greater focus on growth, brand building, customer loyalty and best-in-class service. That is what converts *customers* into *FANS*.

11
Hire for Attitude, Train for Skill

We are there to save money for consumers, not to sell them products they don't need … The key is not to make the sale. The key is to cultivate the customer.

Bernie Marcus, co-founder, The Home Depot

When we recruit, the first question we ask is, "Are you really as committed as we are to win?"

When I visited London banks for the first time in the Holborn area, walking up and down the high street there, all the existing banks I entered were awful. I walked in and I couldn't easily find customer service people. Everyone that I did encounter was dour, employees and customers alike. The ground floor is typically a bank of computers and ATMs and hidden away in the back is where the teller line is. Find a bank employee to help you and you win the game. (But the prize is no prize.)

Need to do something more complicated than make a deposit or cash a cheque? Up a flight of stairs is usually where the new account desks are. At one location, I found a woman who stood out. (She may have appeared brighter than the rest just by comparison.) We talked for a few minutes and I thought she was great, so I gave her one of my cards. "That was great service," I said, "give us a ring about a job."

We look for men and women who are natural born retailers that may have been hiding in banks.

When we're in hiring mode, we're looking for what we call "M Factors": personality and attitude. What kind of zest and excitement do you bring to the retail stores?

We don't care how good you are at maths if you're not a nice person with whom to talk and interact.

Not that it is a surprise to a job applicant; we share with them our smile chart so that they think about it. If you're not smiling when you're trying to get the job, what's the likelihood of you smiling when you're working as a teller at a loud drive-thru on Sunday at 3pm?

One of our biggest challenges is to make sure we continue hiring the right people. Some people like the comfort of 9 to 5 hours, being told what to do, punching the clock, and not making waves. Most bankers have risen in an environment where, if you keep your head down and don't say the wrong thing, a job in banking is almost an entitlement. That's not the attitude *we* look for. Sometimes it takes a while to convince people that working harder than they ever have before, and being held accountable at a higher level than ever before, may be right for them.

"We train people differently at Metro Bank," says CEO Craig Donaldson. "We say their job is to go the extra mile. We reward them for traveling the extra mile and we make them feel special when they do something that creates fans. We recruit people who know what they want to achieve and that's great, great customer service. And that's not something that you put onto a recruiting poster. It's not something that you say. It's something you genuinely believe in and you genuinely live. And my job is to be the most extreme because I've got to be the one who leads this and makes sure that everybody knows that's what they have got to do."

He continues, "It's very simple. It's setting expectations and helping people feel good when they achieve them. We truly have a culture that wants to create fans and wants to do the right thing for customers. We keep the business of banking simple and focused on what it should be."

We believe in a simple hiring formula: if you've got the right attitude toward a job, we can teach you the skills. But if you don't have the right attitude for the fast-moving customer-centric culture that our growing bank represents, we can't teach you a thing.

When hiring for a wide array of customer-facing positions, we often prefer men and women who were not already in banking. Existing bankers often bring too many bad habits, too much baggage, too many stupid rules. We like retail people, folk who already put the customer first.

It is not uncommon for my wife Shirley or me to be out somewhere and receive extraordinary service, and then invite that person to call in about a job with us.

*

Hire for Attitude, Train for Skill is our mantra.

If somebody walks in for a job interview and they don't smile within the first two minutes—we call it the "Smile Trial"—we don't hire them. Because if they want a job and they're walking in and not smiling, what in the world would make us think they will smile at a customer?

Great business models make good colleagues great. Our job is to make sure that they have sufficient resources, tools, and knowledge to do a job and do it in an excellent manner. Training, learning, and continuous development are a huge part of achieving it.

We focus on the things that will make a difference in the customer service experience. This means making sure that our culture of excellence is spread through every single bit of training, that every single day we deliver, so that those messages are reinforced and our people truly do understand this culture of customer service excellence and performance excellence.

Not everybody can or should work at Metro. It is not a typical bank. It is a retailer providing financial products and services. That is what we do, so our job is to make sure that our customers walk away not just satisfied but very, very happy. Employees must understand clearly what our offering is, what our value proposition is, why customers should bank with us.

We sometimes get into trouble when an employee dealing with a customer problem he or she can't appropriately solve doesn't bump it up, or actually creates a stupid rule because the bank that employee came from had a rule for them to hide behind.

At Metro Bank, we're creating a new breed of proud people—customers and employees alike. At Commerce, people had an enormous amount of pride in working for the company because they knew, far and away, that we were the best.

If you have a cashier background, that's fine. But we look more closely at what you have done in the customer service area. Are you smart enough to learn our systems and gain knowledge? Then we put you through extensive training and you have to pass tests in order to make it to the front line. Once you get to the front line, you're observed once a month and given feedback.

The most important thing is having the right attitude, the right "can do" spirit. We want to make things better around you every day. We don't want you to just come into work and go home again in the evening. It's your attitude that's important. We can train you to deal face-to-face with customers, chat over the computer, answer the phone, and come up with the right things to say.

The "Hire for Attitude, Train for Skill" philosophy underpins our whole recruiting effort.

One of the things we have been able to do is develop a lot of people for the bank. As we grow into markets outside London they have the opportunity, if they want to relocate, to bring our culture to those new areas. We can complement the people we hire from these areas—areas that have what I call market equity—with people who really understand our culture and our brand.

*

As Metro Bank has grown in the UK, so has our educational organization. (The original Commerce University, in New Jersey, was modeled on the Disney Institute; the Walt Disney folk invited us in and were generous with their advice in shaping our original corporate training center.)

Metro University offers 71 different classroom courses—yes, 71!

If you say you hire for attitude and train for skill, you'd jolly well better do it.

We have constructed multiple Metro Bank University teaching facilities alongside certain stores to facilitate both new employee training and continuing education programs, so that we can grow the next generation of managers and leaders from within. The main facility is in Holborn, but there are a growing number of satellite centers—including Wimbledon—to reduce travel time.

Classes are taught in person as well as online. And, unlike some organizations, we pay our colleagues their regular salaries while they attend Metro Bank classes.

Once hired, a new colleague will go through the Visions and Values classes. Visions is an introduction to who we are. It's not about process or procedure or even products—it is about our past, our present, our future, and our vision. It is the atmosphere in which new hires will learn the necessary behaviors to execute and deliver our brand of amazing customer service. It's also a fun day in which we want to get them excited to join the

Metro Bank team so that they, in turn, will make our customers happy.

For cashiers and customer service representatives (CSRs), Visions is followed by job training, which will entail several weeks of study and practice—in the classroom and later in the stores. That's the how-to. There are also ancillary computer courses in Microsoft Word and Excel.

The course offerings will expand and grow with the bank—in the pipeline are career development and mentoring programs.

*

On the commercial banking side of staffing it's somewhat different, because when we're hiring lenders, we expect them to have a certain amount of lending and credit experience. The level of skill they bring with them depends on the position that we're offering, such as a real estate or health care lender, or whether it requires the ability to analyze credit relationships. Still, even lender candidates must have the Metro Bank attitude. They have to embrace our corporate, lending and credit culture.

You could be knocking the hide off the ball as a business development person, but if you're not exhibiting the core competencies that we have decided as an organization we want to have, you may score an "A" in your production, but you'll rate a "D" in your competencies because you're not doing it the right way. These characteristics are all taken seriously at Metro Bank.

In some cases, it becomes a challenge because someone who previously worked in a different bank will say, "This is the way I used to do it." However they did it, *we* don't do it that way.

It's even more vital when we hire people who are the equivalent or maybe a little bit higher than our local directors. "This is the way that we used to do it at Barclays." That's nice, but you're not going to get all your leads for business development at Metro Bank from somebody to whom you have to pay a fee.

Pete Musumeci's Story

I was born and raised in Swedesboro, New Jersey. When I graduated from Manhattan College in Riverdale, the Bronx, in 1972, I moved back home and went to work for the local bank in Swedesboro. Two years later, I started with Commerce.

I began as a junior loan officer, primarily making consumer loans. I always reported to Vernon directly—not just then but for my entire career. He was the CEO and loan officer, but as I progressed under him, I rose to senior lender. In 1991, the bank had reached a size at which we needed to split that role in two, and I became the newly created senior credit officer.

In the years that followed, if there was a position open, Vernon wasn't afraid to gamble on people. If he really believed in that person, and he saw skill and talent levels that impressed him as well as a strong work ethic and commitment to the Commerce culture, he wasn't afraid to let them grow into the job—he certainly did that with me. That's one of the best things I can tell you about my 30-year Commerce journey. He always seeks out the person whose potential matches up with an opportunity.

He would take a chance with them and see if they could grow into it. I later did the same thing when I filled positions. With an organization like ours, understanding the culture and how we do business are equally important. There's a lot to be said for somebody who has a pretty good understanding of that culture, and putting them in a position where they're not quite ready and let them grow into it because they have the necessary intangibles. The culture is ingrained in them. They work in it. They understand it and recognize its unique characteristics, as opposed to somebody from outside the organization who may have all the technical skills, but does not have the intangible understanding of the culture that an insider has.

I went to London to help create the commercial side of Metro Bank. My job was to instill our commercial and lending culture with relationship banking. We've taken a world-renowned model and shown that it works anywhere. It's a continuation of all the great things Commerce was about, redoing them in a new market: service, people dealing with people, relationship banking. It's not one of these sophisticated models that get all the big banks in trouble. Every customer we talk to in London says this is what they want, this is the way they want banking to be. This model is very, very portable.

At Commerce—and now at Metro Bank—if you can grasp what the model and the culture is about and if you can get your arms around it, there's no ceiling to where you can go with it.

I changed and grew as my job changed and grew. I learned to do things I never dreamed I could when I joined the company—including helping Vernon create and build an entirely new bank, Metro, in London. I'm an example of a guy whose job evolved and who grew to meet it.

People need to understand that our value proposition is "go out and sell it." Why would we pay a lead-generation fee to somebody else when we can walk straight into a business, talk to an owner or manager, and convince them that we have a better way?

Joining Metro Bank is all about breaking those bad habits, erasing all the stupid rules.

*

During the 11 years that Steve Jobs was exiled from Apple (1985–96), he led NeXT Computer and eventually acquired what became Pixar from George Lucas for a pittance—the sale of the century in Hollywood. That time eventually proved extremely profitable financially, but before that happened, Jobs still had a great deal to learn about how business works and where opportunity sometimes hides. He told biographer Walter Isaacson:

> When I went to Pixar, I became aware of a great divide. Tech companies don't understand creativity. They don't appreciate intuitive thinking, like the ability of an A&R guy at a music label to listen to a hundred artists and have a feel for which five might be successful. And they think that creative people just sit around on couches all day and are undisciplined, because they've not seen how driven and disciplined the creative folks at places like Pixar are. On the other hand, music companies are completely clueless about technology. They think they can just go out and hire a few tech folks. But that would be like Apple trying to hire people to produce music. We'd get second-rate A&R people, just like music companies ended up with second-rate tech people. I'm one of the few people who understands how producing technology requires intuition and creativity, and how producing something artistic takes real discipline.

This ties in with my theory that people reinvent things. People who succeed are lucky that their job uses their special unique talent. We brought high-impact retailing into the banking business, first at Commerce and now at Metro Bank. Jobs said that the tech companies and the music companies never talked to each other until iTunes came along. Similarly, bankers and retailers were never on the same page before Commerce and Metro Bank brought them together.

If you fit the culture of a company and have the necessary technical skills and appropriate work ethic, your potential to grow in a company such as Metro Bank could be unlimited. It's obviously governed by the growth and needs of the company, but we always prefer to promote and hire from within.

One of the things that affects promotion from within is whether there is somebody readily available to replace *you*. What have you done to grow your own successor? That's your responsibility and something unique within smart companies. If you want to move up, we need to replace you, and we prefer to do that from within, so what have you done to accelerate the process?

We have always told people that ours are entrepreneurial companies. "It is *your* company and we want you to look at it as if it was your company." The way people really made money at Commerce and Metro in particular was with stock options, so it was important that they understood our culture.

Employees can look around at any one of our companies and see numerous examples of people who were promoted from within.

You need a high level of integrity to work in our company and you must play well with others because we don't want any type of political environment—it just gets in the way. We customize solutions for our customers. We're nimble. We're here for our customers. Neither employees nor clients will get caught up in a lot of red tape. We can make decisions very, very quickly, internally and externally. If that's the kind of service you want as an employee or a customer, we're the business for you.

Achieve your potential—that's exactly what we do for people. We're constantly looking for colleagues to work alongside us who can appreciate that and dream that. Such people are few and far between, but we've been incredibly fortunate in being able to get a team behind us who can see it and who believe it.

*

The infectious energy found in a Metro Bank store is entirely focused on the customer. Everyone feels a part of it and wants to make a difference in their day.

The challenge of being here for many new hires is the pace. A parent might say to a child, "You're a little bit late. Just start pedaling your legs now, as I kick you out the door." When we onboard people we tell them on day one, "Start running now. Because when you get on the Metro treadmill, you already need to be running fast."

It's invigorating for people who were previously engaged in dead-end, dull positions at other companies. We do things here that haven't been done before. We often hear it said, "My worst day here is still better than my best day at Barclays." It's a feeling that you're making a difference and offering customers a choice.

*

Most job candidates will leave and tell us the process was fun and engaging. They also understand why we didn't offer them a job.

We're pretty good at the telephone interview. Among people who move on to the "M Factor" interview, we offer a job to roughly 80 percent. If you don't get a job at that point, we tell you why. We give you the feedback.

The next step in the process is two days of Visions training, then classes at Metro University for cashiers or CSRs for up to three weeks of pretty intense classroom-based training. If somebody really should not move forward with us, the trainers usually spot it. It's quite rare, but the trainers look for obvious signs, such as lateness, or not appearing to be happy, or an inability to follow basic instructions about how to engage with whatever we're talking about in the classroom. We know that we can train people to do the job. But we expect new hires to bring the right attitude, to be positive, and to smile.

Where it's more of a challenge is if we're filling a highly technical IT or accountant job. They not only need a specific set of skills, but they also have to fit the Metro culture. If they don't, they're not going to be happy here. Trying to assess people through the lens of their experience and their competence, while at the same time keeping an eye on culture and behaviors, is tricky. I wish I could say that we never get it wrong, but that's the area where we sometimes do. People who have worked in big, formal, bureaucratic institutions don't always understand the need to work collaboratively. We have processes and systems, controls and governances, because we're a bank. But we don't have an unnecessary, legacy bureaucracy.

*

A couple of years ago we had someone in the commercial banking team doing property lending. It worried us that he worked very much on his own. We have relationship managers who tend to deal with existing customers. And then there are credit partners and credit analysts who support the commercial lenders in putting together deals and submitting them to a credit committee, depending on the size of the deal. But this lender wanted to work on his own. At the end of the year, he was given his performance and behavior review rating.

"Your delivery is exceptional," his supervisor said. "Your behavior as a member of the team, however, is not great. You tend to want to work as an individual, but that is not the way the bank operates."

The lender was then told what his variable, year-end reward would be. It was much lower than he expected.

"But I've delivered millions of pounds worth of business for the bank," he responded.

"Yes, but you haven't done it on your own. You did it with all the infrastructure that sits behind you."

He couldn't comprehend that he was part of a team.

"You can have your bonus," his supervisor said, "but you need to leave because you're not happy here. And you don't want to work as part of a team. If what's important to you is just what you achieve and your cash reward for that, there are other places where you'll be much happier than here."

That was quite difficult for the supervisor because the man was a really good lender. But when people aren't happy in a role, you can see it. And it's really poisonous.

*

There are, naturally, always a few people who don't fit in despite our best efforts to weed them out during the earliest stages of the onboarding process.

I'd love to say it never happens. But since it does, I'm proud to say that we deal with it. We encourage them to go find happiness elsewhere. This isn't a good place to be if you don't fit, because you stand out from a mile away.

One of the reasons people don't fit is that they are unable to put Metro Bank and the team first. Often they've worked in organizations where it was all about bureaucracy, managing their career, making sure they are okay first. When they come here, we say, "No one's going to push you under a bus. You need to think about your job differently. You need to think about it the Metro way. You're not listening to us. You're not grasping the model. That's not how we do it."

Typically, it is people who've been in big, bureaucratic, clunky organizations for their whole career, especially if they've only been in one business. If they've always been at a British cartel bank and have experienced only one culture—and only one way of doing things—to come here where it's so different can be a struggle if they're not the right people.

We have controls and processes. We're a regulated

organization. But we don't have the common British bureaucracy that drags other companies in the UK to a grinding halt.

We work in the background to turn the complex into the simple, so that any issue represents complexity for the few and simplicity for the many. We use language that reinforces our culture.

For example, we want to treat our colleagues fairly and we want to support them, but we also expect them to behave in the right way. Our attendance guidelines say we expect you to come to work when you can, because it has a real impact if you don't. We say that in straightforward, sensible language, which a lot of organizations run away from. They're more concerned about legally nailing it down. Why? It's reasonable to ask people to come to work if they can. And it's reasonable to tell them what the impact will be if they don't.

We reinforce it everywhere, because what we say to our people and what they read while they're at work, and what they hear while they're at work, is the language they will use with our customers. If we use complex, legalistic, negative, preventative language, that's what they will use with our customers. We don't want that to happen because how we treat people is how they behave. We're clear that the internal language we use is as important as the external language we use on a sign in one of our store windows.

*

We put on lots of public events and encourage people from other businesses to visit us, and we talk to them about what we do and how we do it. They say to me, "Aren't you worried that we're going to replicate what you do at our place?" And I say, "Go ahead. Please try! Because you won't be as obsessive as we are about it."

As you discovered in Chapter 9, the first "A" of AMAZE(ing) stands for "Attend to every detail."

If you speak to our recruiters and ask, "What's your job?", they will answer, "We're supposed to find the right people who are a great cultural fit and brilliantly talented." But pretty quickly after that, they'll say, "And to give the most positive candidate experience whether we hire people or not, so that they leave as fans."

Few enterprises can get that alignment out of everybody in support of the company goal, creating an environment where people feel supported and empowered to do that. We hire amazing people and explain to the ones that aren't amazing that they should go and find somewhere they'll fit. British organizations lack the gumption to be so direct.

*

We also do "friends and family" hiring, where anyone who introduces someone to join the bank gets a £500 thank you after the new employee has been with us for six months.

Research showed us that friends and family hires stay twice as long—and perform better—because they understand what they're joining. A colleague will not introduce someone who will let them down. They want good people working around them if they care about the organization. And if they're not engaged with the organization, they won't introduce new people anyway. We pay out on 15–20 percent of our new hires. (It would probably be even higher, but our executives don't participate in the scheme.)

What is the most important thing we do? We listen to the voice of the customer. If we stop putting that at the heart of everything we do, we become just like every other bank.

12

Hope is Not a Plan

If anyone is going to destroy our online shopping business model, it's going to be us.

Jeff Bezos, founder, Amazon

If anyone is going to reinvent British banking, it will be us—not because we hope it will happen but because we have the culture and the model, and are fanatical about execution.

People say to me, "I hope I get this deal." Or, "I hope she comes to work for us." "I hope he takes our loan commitment." "I hope we make our budget."

The list of declarations that start "I hope" goes on forever and I always end up saying, "Let's not hope about it. Go out and *make* it happen."

When people use the word *hope*, they're basically saying they don't have control. What I want to know is how are *you* going to make something happen? As a business plan, hope is not at all useful. We want to recruit people where hope is not a plan.

Don't dream about execution—*execute*!

We understand who we are, what we are and what we can accomplish. In other words, we don't *think* we're going to do something, we *know* we are.

Here's a relevant thought on this subject from Larysa Slobodian, a blogger and principal consultant at L4 Leadership:* "It is wonderful to have hope, but hope is not a plan and cannot dictate change on its own. And, sometimes, hope can be the undercover agent for denial."

What gets measured gets done! That has a lot to do with the building up of pipelines for new customers on both the retail and commercial sides of Metro Bank. When we talk about reporting and holding our people accountable, it means talking to them regularly. What else do you need? Do you need someone higher up to come in and help you close this deal? Do you need the chief executive to meet a client? Because let me tell you, being able to deliver that is incredibly powerful in our business. When we walk around at an opening and talk to people for hours and hours, we hear it's an access to the top not available at the main London high street banks. At Metro Bank, our customers will see the founder and CEO of the bank quite often.

If an account officer says, "If we do this loan, we *hope* to get all of the customer's deposit business," that's not the right approach. It should be, "If we do this loan, we *will* get all the deposit business."

We have great products, we have great people, we have great locations, so to the physical extent that we are able to handle the customer's deposit needs, we must believe we will get all the business, not just "hope" to get *all* the business.

We need to have a realistic basis for believing that our model will produce more business, not just "hope" it's going to produce more business.

*

* "When Does Rescue Turn Into Recovery?", February 10, 2011, L4 Leadership blog by Larysa Slobodian, www.l4leadership.com/l4/executive/when-does-rescue-turn-into-recovery/

Hope is not a plan. You've got to plan and you've got to put the right things in place to deliver it. You've also got to base your plans in fact and in delivery.

Somebody will say, "I went to see a customer and I'm hoping they're going to come back to me."

And I'll say, "What have you done since then? When are you going back to them? Why would the customer have to come back to you? It's your job to make their life easier. How does them coming back to you make their life easier?"

"They wanted to think about it. They said they'd get back to me."

"So your plan is that you hope they'll get back to you? Hope is a plan now, is it?"

In the real world of chasing and developing business, you've got to have a realistic plan. You've got to take ownership and think, "How can I make life easy for customers?" That's the key.

We see this on both sides of the bank, consumer and commercial. Businesses need help; they need things to happen for them. Things certainly happen *to* them.

*

We're always looking to improve.

We took our original retail bank and we grew it every year in the US. Then we took the central model to a completely different market an ocean away and, lo and behold, it is a gigantic success because the principles are universal for successful retail businesses.

Every successful business must eliminate "hope" from its vocabulary and install model, execution and success in its place. Entrepreneurs make things happen; they don't wait for miracles.

There are plenty of differences between American business practices and those of the British. And there's no doubt that the "can do" American culture clashes with the "let's study it"

British approach. The London media and business establishment asks us all the time why there has not been a new British high street bank in 100-plus years.

The real answer is a reluctance to challenge the status quo.

In our job interview process at Metro Bank (and Commerce before), certain candidates will move up the ladder and meet a variety of officers and executives, depending on the vacancy. At some point, someone will ask the candidate, "Do you understand the Metro model? Do you understand the lending culture and the credit culture and all that?" They invariably say, "Yes" and we will invariably say, "No, you don't." You don't have any idea what it's all about until you've been here and you've lived it and breathed it.

When you hire, does the applicant understand and buy into your model and culture?

A lot of men and women come to us from banks where the only way they could compete for customers was on price, whether that means interest rates, loan structure, loan terms or accepting a lack of guarantees. They could compete only by making it easier for the customer, compared with what other banks were offering. That's not how *we* compete. We never compete on price and we never compete on credit standards. We compete on everything that we do: the entire service mentality; the way every corner of the Metro Bank business works together; how we have an account officer who handles all of a customer's needs; how we will introduce the customer to the credit officer, senior management, or the local branch manager.

Many job candidates come to us believing that shaving half a point off a customer's existing rate or extending a loan by four years will close loans. We're not built that way. We compete on service, service, and more service.

We ask the candidate, "Have you heard anything different from the four or five people you spoke to?" And the answer is always "No" because we're consistent in our beliefs and our actions.

The word "control" is important at Metro Bank. How do we control the relationship? What's the hot button for the customer? What do they really need? What do they really want?

When we have control of the relationship—and we don't mean control in the sense that we will tell a customer how to run their business—when we understand what they need, we're positioning them to succeed because of the way the bank can help them. At times, that might mean saying "No" because the bank can't do something, or maybe what the customer wants isn't the right thing. They might not realize it, but maybe it isn't the right path or choice. When we have that kind of control of the relationship, it helps to solidify things and get business done a lot quicker and smarter.

We've been consistent for 40-plus years in the firm belief that *hope is not a plan*. Don't merely hope things will work out— have a real, executable plan of action!

*

Many of the British citizens we've met are a little bit like New Yorkers: skeptical!

When we first went into New York and announced that Commerce would be open seven days a week, New Yorkers were dubious. "Okay," they said, "that will last six months, tops." And they reserved judgment for good reason: previous banks had not lived up to what they said they would do. Even the ones that tried to copy us by saying, "We're going to extend our hours and be open on Saturdays in some locations" ultimately backed off.

When we really do what we say we will do and are consistent about our commitment to convenience and loving our customers, they love us unconditionally and become fans. And then they tell their friends. As everybody knows, the best recommendation is a one-to-one when somebody says, "Oh my, the bank just screwed that up again for you? Switch to my bank!"

*

At the opening of the first Metro Bank store in Holborn, people would come in tentatively, ask some questions, take some literature, and come back later to open an account.

As the next few stores opened, we saw that behavior evolve. Now people were bringing a passport. They were ready to do business immediately. They might say, "Tell me more about Metro Bank," but they were sitting down at a team member's desk to open an account while asking their questions.

In the latest stores that we've opened, they're on their mobile phones before walking out with their new cheques and debit cards, calling their friends and telling them to come over and join them. I have seen the same person come back three times during an opening weekend, each time bringing more friends and family.

Metro Bank is catching on in London even quicker than Commerce did in Manhattan. After five years, we're hearing the same thing we did at Commerce: "When are you going to be in *my* neighborhood?"

13

Design as a Competitive Weapon

Design is the fundamental soul of a human-made creation that ends up expressing itself in successive outer layers of the product or service.

Steve Jobs, co-founder, Apple

Go ahead: judge our bank by its cover.

According to Walter Isaacson, author of the biography *Steve Jobs*, Apple stores average 5,400 customer visits a week. That's a stellar number for any retailer.

But if that's great business traffic, consider *this* number: Commerce Bank stores everywhere averaged 12,000 customers a week in 2006!

Our store is our public face. Metro Bank, our lifeline to the customer, is the reincarnation of the *FANS not customers* model for banking and we know it will reach explosive traffic numbers in short order.

Like us, Jobs believed the best places for his retail stores were always the highest trafficked locations available. He believed the Apple stores should be in high-end malls and on high streets, areas with a lot of foot traffic, no matter how expensive the cost per square foot. *He and I both believe the best site is almost always worth the price.*

"We may not be able to get them to drive ten miles to check out our products, but we can get them to walk ten feet," he told Walter Isaacson. Microsoft Windows users, in particular, had to be ambushed. "If they're passing by, they will drop in out of curiosity, if we make it inviting enough, and once we get a chance to show them what we have, we will win."

Jobs went on to say, "In most people's vocabularies, design means veneer. It's interior decorating. It's the fabric of the curtains or the sofa. But to me, nothing could be further from the meaning of design. *Design is the fundamental soul of a human-made creation that ends up expressing itself in successive outer layers of the product or service.*" (Emphasis added.)

At Commerce, and now at Metro Bank, the look and the location and the design of our stores are a direct reflection of the brand and are an important element in communicating the brand. I scouted and picked all the locations at Commerce and make all the final decisions at Metro Bank. Shirley and her team design the facilities to reinforce the brand.

Shirley is the keeper of the brand. You can see her touch in the big things, like the design of our buildings, inside and out. But it's also found in a multitude of smaller things, from desks and door handles to pens and dog bandanas. I couldn't have created the culture, look, and feel of these businesses without her contributions.

Successful retailing is all about details. How your store looks inside, how the products and services are presented, how your people look—these are all part of your brand. We constantly look at the height of ceilings, lighting levels, even how to best use the store floor itself. There isn't one thing in the presentation of the Metro Bank brand that wasn't thought about, from what you see every step up to and through the front doors. What can you see? Is it fun?

Shirley's entire career was fashioned around the ideas of Frank Lloyd Wright: design from the inside out. Her winning approach comes from knowing who will occupy a building and then making it a point of destination for that particular client from the outside: the signage, the materials, what the building itself looks like and how it looks on the site. But then, from the inside, she focuses on how it will operate. She feels that the culture of a business can be affected by its environment.

Shirley once created a call center headquarters for a large insurance company in the US. She insisted that it should be glass enclosed, and that it should avoid low ceilings and terrible lighting—all common, low-cost approaches to such facilities. Her concept was that it should be one of the *best* places environmentally, not an oversized closet, because when its staff picked up the phone to answer a customer's call, all the company had going for it was the representative's voice and attitude. She made the case that their attitude could be shaped by their surroundings, how they feel about themselves and the space in which they're working.

Customer service is a life's work. I learned, over the years, to trust Shirley's judgment, knowing that she would accurately interpret the look and feel of our brands. She knows—even when I don't. She knows the secret recipe: which colors are happy and which are drab; why one thing is round over here and has an angle over there.

Sometimes you can spot Shirley's touch in the tiniest details—like the millions of free Metro Bank pens we give away at every opportunity. In 2007, Commerce Bank gave away 28 million pens. She and her InterArch team even won an award for their design of a water bottle during the Commerce days.

As for pens, most banks go to great lengths to chain theirs to desks and counters so customers can't steal them. Why? We have always wanted customers to *take* our brightly colored pens, embossed with the Metro Bank logo. Need one? It's yours. Need five? Share them with your friends and, along the way, help us spread our name around. Talk about making an impression!

When Shirley and her staff designed the pens, they considered their weight, how they looked and how they felt. We didn't pick one out of a catalogue; we designed them from the inside out.

*

Retail design is more important than it ever has been as we are visually bombarded with information every second of every day.

We want you to know when you walk through Metro Bank's doors or encounter us via a brochure or an event or online that life is different at Metro. The experience is everything.

We build large sheets of street-facing glass in our store windows that let customers see in, in brightest day or darkest night. We think our stores look better at night than they do in the daytime because you can really see inside at night. They're open and architecturally carved by the lighting. The finishes are all high-end. It's impossible to look in our windows or walk through our doors without seeing people smiling.

Traditional British banks have limited hours, they're dirty, they're not attractive, and they don't attract customers.

*

As I have for the past 40 years, I turned to my wife Shirley to develop our Metro Bank and brand.

In the UK, Shirley is doing even more at Metro than she did at Commerce. She directs the architectural design and the construction, but she is also the marketing leader and keeper of the brand.

Design is one of the core business basics at Metro Bank, from the bright red color that represents the brand everywhere you find it, to the big windows and the architectural lighting in the stores, day or night. Our desks are wood, not laminate, because that's where the customer sits, sending a clear message about how we feel about them. The flooring design is functional—*directional*—guiding customers in and about.

We started designing Metro Bank locations from the entry point, and it's a fun process, quite energizing. The focus is on thinking about someone else rather than ourselves.

The environment is crucial. It's not one thing, it's the sum of all the parts that creates the customer experience. When I walk through the door is the space open, is it friendly, is it bright, is it inviting? Is everything in excellent condition? Is there any clutter making things look messy? Does someone walk up and smile at me and say "Hello" and welcome me? When they give me a tour of the store and listen to my concerns and needs, do they know which product or service will improve my life? When I leave, am I thanked for my business?

The idea is to create a customer for life. If we fail on a lot of these components, we won't have that customer for life, will we? The way we continue to service that customer on a day-in and day-out basis is what makes us winners.

If you think about it, it's not too hard to figure out how you would *like* to be treated in a bank, and that's what Shirley is great at doing. You don't want to wait in line forever; you want the store to be open when you can get there. And the Metro Bank logo is seen behind the cashiers so you know without a doubt where you are.

Any successful retail business develops a unique, engaging, and fun environment. That is what turns customers into fans—every time.

*

Integration delivers a total, consistent message.

Shirley and InterArch handle the same things at Metro Bank that they did at Commerce, but here she oversees architectural design, construction management, and the marketing and brand architecture of the bank. She's united architecture, design, marketing and branding.

She is the brand queen, and she is in total control of the look and feel.

The *Daily Mail* wrote a story about how *Shirley doesn't let me design banks, and I don't let her sign cheques.* It's a perfect fit, professionally and personally.

We don't let anyone change so much as a form letter unless Shirley approves it, because we've got thousands of colleagues who previously worked for the big four British banks and who might bring in old habits.

We like to tell people that Shirley is rebuilding Britain, one town at a time.

*

Shirley said that the first two stores we opened—Holborn and Earl's Court—design-wise were what she would call two of her more understated designs.

"I say 'understated' because it was a big enough leap for the market at the time, between the architecture and culture," she said. "I think I have, since then, become known for my ceilings and different effects that we do in the bank, as well as the volume of the space, and how it feels outside and inside. It all has the same language. There's a Metro architectural language, but each one is different in how those parts are put together."

Everyone told us the design wouldn't work in London, that people wouldn't come in and sit next to each other and actually talk about opening an account, giving details and everything. They would *never* do that. They had to have more privacy! How could the British do business in the open? Cashiers with no glass? And the vivid colors of the Magic Money Machine? They said, "You need to do pastels. A bank needs to be very, very quiet on the ears and the eyes."

But we came to start a revolution. And you don't start a revolution quietly!

Our basic colors are red, white, and blue. In the early days, many Brits complained that we were using "American colors."

Shirley had a ready answer: "Have you ever looked at the Union Jack? It's red, white, and blue. America *copied* the red, white, and blue. The English went into battle wearing bright red coats, remember?"

People forget that. The reality is, our colors couldn't be more British. Some early reviews in the press said the stores felt like a Las Vegas casino. That's all settled down, for the most part, and customers and employees alike are proud of the stores, which gives Shirley and me a lot of enjoyment.

It's impossible to walk through our front door, look around, be greeted immediately by a smiling colleague who says "Can I help you?" and not know that life is different here.

*

Shirley tells our colleagues all the time that they're rock stars.

"Do you know you're a rock star?" she said. "Don't you feel a little different? Do your friends look at you a little differently? You're working for Metro Bank!"

*

Shirley and her design team sometimes have to bend to meet local government council requirements, just as they did in the United States. Shirley finds ever more creative ways to match the Metro Bank design language to community standards. Sometimes they don't want us to use metal panels or they want render on the outside of the building. In Aylesbury, where we opened a new store in 2015, we rebuilt a town square that was also home to all of our competition. We stand out there like a beacon, bright and welcoming—the antithesis of the gloom and disinterest of the other banks.

In Brighton, we basically built a building within a building. The original structure had a famous dome on the top. Shirley took the dome off and put it back, fully restored, when construction was finished.

A growing number of locations, as we expanded into the suburbs of London, are in shopping malls and town centers.

Some older British buildings present unique engineering and construction challenges.

"We go in thinking we have a good idea of what we'll find," Shirley said, "but there are often surprises. I thought I was surprised in New York, when we were only dealing with 100-year-old buildings. But in Britain, you're dealing with centuries of history. Nothing is the same-old, same-old. Commerce Bank construction in the suburbs of New Jersey was much more cookie-cutter in nature. Vernon found a piece of ground and, depending on the topography, maybe the drive-thru had to change orientation. But it was pretty much the same. But when we're going into existing UK space that has been fitted and refitted over and over for hundreds of years, it's a whole different ballgame. We have to have a flexible engineering and architectural team."

One of Shirley's favorite designs is the standalone store in Southall, our second store with a drive-thru teller line. It's at the outer edge of a shopping center and looks more like a modern glass museum than a bank.

As much as possible, Shirley gives each store its own personality.

Design is our competitive weapon.

*

The first Metro Bank stores in London were built in the United States and shipped by container for on-site assembly. Shirley did it that way to maintain quality standards until we found crafts-men who met her expectations in Britain.

We now have local engineers and builders that meet Shir-ley's exacting standards and understand what we expect. Only the vault and safe deposit boxes are still manufactured in the US. We've been able to source 90 percent of our stone, columns and wood from the UK and Europe. Some of the furniture comes from Canada.

"I had a double nemesis," Shirley said. "I had to have high quality in shortened timeframes. It was nothing when we landed here for contractors to say it would take 14 months to build a new store. And 'yes' from a contractor meant 'maybe.' They felt that as long as they made a good effort, if they missed a deadline they should not be held responsible or accountable. They behaved as though accountability was a gray area because 'We tried.' Our model requires results, not just showing up. This isn't grade school football where all the children get a trophy for participation. Metro Bank can't miss a grand opening date; this is a for-profit enterprise, not a lesson in self-esteem. It was a mindset that I didn't accept. As a result, there were contractors who said to my face, 'We don't want to build for you.' So it took time to build a cadre of builders and engineers. We had to kiss a lot of frogs, as the saying goes."

*

When we opened in Aylesbury, Shirley went round to shop the competition, dressed in Metro Bank red, but minus the usual Metro "M" pin on her lapel.

She started at HSBC, where the lobby was half the size of our ATM vestibule—extremely small. There were two cashiers behind glass, and a third woman seated at a desk. She saw a couple of machines and stopped to read brochures, looking at this, looking at that.

"Can I help you?" the woman at the desk asked.

"No, not really," Shirley said. "I'm from Metro Bank. And I'm shopping you."

"Oh, really?"

"Yes, but you should feel free to come shop us, too," Shirley said. "You don't even have to come inside; we have such big glass windows, you can see in easily."

The woman nodded, unsure how to respond.

"What hours are you open?" Shirley asked.

"We're open every weekday and Saturdays from 10am to 2pm."

"Oh, really?"

"Yes," the woman said. "But you can't do any transactions."

"What?" That caught Shirley by surprise. "You're open on Saturdays, but customers can't do any transactions?"

"Oh," she said, "you can use the *machines*."

"Okay. And are you here?"

"Yes—me or someone like me is here. The cashiers, no," the woman said. "It gives us an opportunity to talk to our customers."

"But not serve them?"

"But not serve them."

You just can't make this stuff up, folks.

*

Every month, Shirley visits groups of 60 or more Metro colleagues. She'll ask them questions such as:

- What does "owning" your store mean to you?
- Do you think that asking for business is bad?
- How do you ask for business?
- What's the Metro way of doing this?

Seguso

Seguso Vetri d'Arte is a 600-year-old Italian glass company on the Venetian island of Murano, in which Shirley and I purchased an interest in 2008. My wife loves glass and applies it in big, bold ways to most every structure she designs, but she also loves to collect it as art. I thought it would be an interesting experiment to see if we could apply the *FANS not customers* model to the Seguso family firm.

The early results are mixed; it's a little like changing the wheels on Nero's chariot as it heads into battle.

We've known the family for a long time and bought many stunning works of art from them that brighten both our offices and our homes. They have glass designs that are 600 years old. (Last month's accounting records? Not so much!)

We're essentially attempting to change an entire corporate culture. We started an apprenticeship program to train new artists in the ancient arts. We believe that by selling the emotion and history of the brand we can develop new markets and a greater appreciation for its legacy and beauty.

In this endeavor, I try to imagine how our banking cartel competitors in London would fare trying to adopt our culture to their 1700s business models. (Even if they cared to try!)

As Shirley told the *Financial Times Magazine*'s Lucia van der Post in a November 2015 feature story, we are not just investors, we are business builders.

Can it be done?

Stay tuned.

Near the end of the meetings, Shirley will ask the attendees to send her pictures of the competition, particularly examples of how they do business differently from us.

For example, at a NatWest bank branch, customers were greeted by a red plastic child's stool. On it was a single sheet of paper, with several drawings on it, and a small wicker basket, which should hold crayons—but it was empty. By contrast, our stores are always well supplied with coloring books and crayons for children to occupy their time while their parents do their business.

14

No Stupid Rules

As a company, one of our greatest cultural strengths is accepting the fact that if you're going to invent, you're going to disrupt. A lot of entrenched interests are not going to like it. Some of them will be genuinely concerned about the new way, and some of them will have a vested self-interest in preserving the old way.

Jeff Bezos, founder, Amazon

What is a stupid rule?

Every organization has endless stupid rules. This is often an unintended result of the bureaucracy that is built up to support the business. Stupid rules are a result of misguided or erroneous assumptions about what best serves—or protects—an organization's status quo.

Bankers always tell me that my policies are ridiculous: "You can't open your doors on Sunday, because no one will work on Sunday!"

I think *they're* the ridiculous ones. Every retailer and every mall is open on Sunday, but bankers think a bank branch should operate apart from what is most convenient to its customers. That, my friends, is one stupid rule!

Let's say you get paid with a cheque from your employer's bank. If you don't bank there, if you go in to cash your cheque, they might fingerprint you *and* charge you a fee for the privilege. How does that make sense?

Nobody raises a hand and objects, "How do these rules affect the customer experience for the vast majority of law-abiding bank guests who might be potential customers in the future?"

If we fingerprint a person unnecessarily once, that person will *never* become a customer. That's how stupid rules affect a brand.

One of the things we did throughout the years at Commerce and now do at Metro Bank is to make sure that when we deliver a new product, whatever policies, procedures, and products we create are based on a simple standard. If it can't be explained to our youngest colleagues in a sentence or two, it's too complicated.

It goes back to the essence of Sam Walton, who founded the world's largest, most successful and most profitable retail operation, Wal-Mart. He believed that, in retail sales, you don't have to be 100 percent better than the competition. You only have to be 15 percent better—but you have to get better all the time.

Here are some of my favorite examples of other stupid British bank rules:

* **Make an appointment if you want to open a new account!** Requiring new customers to make an appointment to apply for a current or savings account is a stupid bank rule. You can walk into a Metro Bank seven days a week and open a new current or savings account on the spot (including online banking) in about 15 minutes (or an hour for a commercial account). And we even have "Bank at Work Days" when we go to the workplaces of our business clients and sign up their employees for new accounts on the spot.

- **To open a new account, a bank requires a valid driver's license, passport, utility bills, etc!** Not at Metro Bank. If you're British and you have a valid driver's license or passport, that's all you need at Metro Bank for instant account opening. But at many British banks, you have to come with your utility bills, the lease on your flat, plus a driver's license and/or passport. We eliminated that. We have ways to validate passports and let us know immediately whether they're genuine or not. We put this technology in place to protect ourselves, yet the net result is convenience for our customers.

- **Allow two weeks to issue and/or replace debit and credit cards!** When a private banking customer of one of the London high street cartel banks lost his wallet just before leaving on holiday, he was surprised to find it would take his bank two weeks to replace his debit and credit cards. That would wreck his plans. Someone told him that Metro Bank could print new cards for a customer in any of its stores so he went into one and opened a new account. He left with new cards and a smile on his face. When he returned from his holiday, he transferred *all* his accounts to Metro Bank.

- **All loans must go through the pricing committee!** Some British banks have what they call a "pricing" committee that determines whether a prospective loan is priced properly. Why do I need a committee of people to tell me if a loan is priced properly? Our account officers or credit people know our model and should be able to determine instantly whether we've got a loan properly priced.

- **No bikes in the bank!** For many reasons, our stores are designed to avoid entry stairways. Craig Donaldson, CEO of Metro Bank, discovered how convenient that is early one morning when he encountered a cyclist in one of the stores. The cyclist used to ride past our store every morning on the way to work when he noticed two things: (1) we're open earlier than any other bank in the neighborhood, and (2) because there are no steps at the store's entrance, he could ride his bike in, lean it against the counter, do his business and be on his way. Elsewhere, he'd waste time and energy chaining up his bike outside, doing his banking inside, going back outside, unchaining his bike and going. It's a small thing to a non-cyclist, but it takes time and it mattered to him. He said, "It's brilliant for me. Fantastic."

- **No toys for children whose maths isn't perfect!** A little girl who must have been about four poured loose change into the Magic Money Machine but guessed the amount she entered incorrectly. She started crying because she couldn't have a toy. Of course, we gave her the toy because we want a happy child. The parents were blown away. They said that would have never happened at another bank: "They would have stuck to the rules." The cashier said, "Probably, but we don't want anybody unhappy."

The last story reinforces our "One to say yes, two to say no" rule. It's about our people doing the right thing. Or, more obviously, not doing stupid, detrimental things.

The customer service representative who came to the little girl's rescue told Craig, "In my previous bank I wouldn't have been allowed to do that because she hadn't guessed the right number."

"But she was crying," Craig said. "Wouldn't they just want to make her happy? Wasn't that the right thing to do?"

And she said, "Of course it was, but the process said you had to guess within £1. In my previous bank, I would have been reprimanded: 'Why did you do that? She didn't get it right!' Whereas here I knew it was the right thing to give her the toy, so I did."

And that's the difference. Can you imagine that family with the little girl going home, and the next day her dad telling parents at her school the story? You *know* they talked about it. Or the guy with the bike saying he told all his mates who cycle that they should do their banking at Metro as well. Oh, and if they leave wet or muddy marks on a rainy day, we'll wipe them up. It's not hard to do! Tell me where we lost a penny making these customers—I mean *FANS*—happy!

I always questioned why every retailer painted their delivery vans with their marketing message and brand, but banks did not.

Bank security people fret about protecting the dead cheques they move around every day, causing the branding experts to lose thousands of daily advertising impressions by not marketing their van exteriors. But those dead cheques have no cash value! They move from point to point due to electronic scanning and regulatory requirements, but after that they are garbage. That's why we make our vehicles into unmistakable, rolling adverts for Metro Bank.

If a bank won't paint its vehicles, what *will* it change?

Processes should be followed where they work. Where they don't, they should be challenged as stupid rules.

So many times, good ideas are struck down because they are too hard to execute. "No, they'll never do that, are you kidding?" Can't you just hear a business's operational people saying that?

Some people hear our "No Stupid Rules" philosophy and choose to bank with us for that alone.

Every business should pride itself on running a never-ending campaign to find and kill every stupid rule.

*

Andrew Richards is Metro Bank's Head of Regional Retail Banking. His job is to ensure that the stores smell, taste, feel, sound, and live the model. He has worked with me for 30 years now, starting decades ago at Commerce. We had six stores when he joined us in New Jersey and 440 when I left in 2007.

He is constantly on guard against any stupid bank rules ever creeping in. If he uncovers any, his assignment is to kill them quickly.

Ours was the first new British high street bank in 100-plus years. We employ thousands of people, many of whom worked at one of the British cartel banks at some point before joining us. And almost every one of them grew up with the lousy customer service the cartel banks are renowned for worldwide. As such, some of their history, tradition and stupid rules from other banks sneak in from time to time. Andrew's role is to make sure we stop it at the front door, so to speak.

At every other bank in London, if you want to open up a business account, you have to make an appointment. And for some reason that appointment is generally scheduled weeks away, when the business needs it now. *Right now.* That is a stupid bank rule. At Metro, we're set up so that whether you're a businessperson or a consumer, you don't have to make an appointment to open an account with us. We will open up a new account on the spot, usually within an hour. That's a huge differentiator between us and everyone else.

*

One of the challenges for Metro Bank has been in what we call the "misery-go-round." The UK government measures the number of people using its Current Account Switching Service (CASS). They report, as a measure of success, how many people are using CASS.

To increase their current account numbers, banks will pay customers a bonus: "Join us and we'll give you £100. And if you convince a friend to join us, we'll give you £100 and we'll give them £100." That varies by bank, with some paying as much as £150.

Those switching incentives are being paid for in two ways. One is that they're hitting their loyal customers by reducing their savings rates without telling them. It's legal for banks in the UK to take down their savings rate by one-quarter of a percent. And they can do that *twice* a year.

Talk about a stupid rule!

It's an incentive paid for by hitting the bank's existing customers.

We don't play that game. Instead, we launched a savings promise. The banking cartel cuts rates without telling people so we do the opposite. First of all, we've never cut our rate. If you received a really high interest rate when we opened, you'll still be on that rate. And if we bring out a flexible rate savings product that is higher than the rate you're currently on, we will put you on it automatically, and then we will write to tell you we've done it. That is a promise. That is looking at what the market does, and doing the opposite. We're not going to cut rates without telling you. We're going to raise rates and tell you.

*

Banks aren't the only institutions with customer service challenges in the UK, as Andrew Richards discovered when he relocated here from America.

"It's a culture where the first part of every sentence is, 'It can't be done' or 'No' or 'I'm going to try, but don't expect anything,'" he said of everything from turning on the electricity in his flat for the first time to installing cable television and internet service. "Setting up the cable and internet required a good three-week lead time. In the States, the cable company just sends a box to you via UPS or post. Here, it requires 'specialist' training—and a different specialist each for cable and internet even though both services likely come from the same provider. Each installation was a separate appointment and a separate five-hour window of time spent waiting for a knock on the door.

"They called me the night before the appointments," Andrew continues. "They introduced themselves, and I said, 'Really looking forward to it; I took the time off on Friday.' To which the person on the other end of the line said, 'No, no, no. I'm sorry. I cannot talk to you about this until I've taken you through security.' They wanted to verify that I was the person that they were calling. To which my response was, 'I just want to be clear on something. *You* called *me*. I think we can skip the security step, because we've already jumped that hurdle.

"And that's not atypical."

We feel special pain for anyone moving to the UK from somewhere else. If you're an American or Canadian and you're coming to work for, say, Starbucks in London, UK banks will not open an account for you because you need six months' proof of address history. And they can't get a credit report for you because you have no UK credit history. They don't see American credit histories. A college degree and 20 years of solid credit experience, paying all your bills on time, mean nothing.

Elsewhere, the impact of corporate policies and procedures on the customer is almost an afterthought, rather than the driver of any decision. Fortunately for us, most of the other banks just want to imitate each other. Their view is that there is safety in numbers.

By contrast, we've worked with several American companies so that if they have folk coming here, we will bank them. The British cartel banks won't open accounts for Americans or American companies moving into the UK. Their rules forbid them from taking American business; we welcome them. We say, prove to us that you're employed and show your business ID, and we will establish an account.

British businesses spend a lot of energy on finding a way to say "No."

We work just as hard at saying "*Yes.*"

My View

William C. Taylor

Co-founder, Fast Company *magazine, and author,* Mavericks At Work

Commerce Bank stood out when I was doing research for my book *Mavericks At Work* because what they were doing was so rare and virtually nonexistent in the banking business.

Something Vernon said to me, which has stuck with me, is that "Every great company has re-imagined the industry that it's in."

I think if you look at the Commerce Bank story, they rethought and re-imagined the sense of what was possible in the financial services business. First, what could it mean to be a bank? Psychologically and emotionally, what could the experience for a customer be encountering an institution which is part of the day-to-day fabric of life after all? Second, from the point of view of the strategy with which you compete in the business, the business model with which you go to market, could you rethink and re-imagine a lot of the traditional logic of how banks make money, what banks think are important in terms of the deposits they're gathering and the loans they're making or whatever the case may be?

And so what really struck me about Commerce Bank more than anything was that there was an ironclad connection with the economic value proposition. That is to say the strategy and the costs and the ways of operating around which the business was built, and the human values proposition, the culture, the experience, the design, and the sensibility that customers encountered day-to-day doing business.

I think that magical connection between economic value and human values is really, in some sense, what informs most really great companies and most really great brands—we certainly see it with Apple in computing. We see it with Four Seasons in hospitality, and who would think we would see it in the banking world as well?

That's what really made me sit up and take notice of Commerce Bank.

A lot of what I do is look at very successful organizations and the strategy they use to create economic value, and the culture and approach to innovation they use to compete on human values. It strikes me that for many, many years of their long run, there was such clarity in the minds of Vernon, his senior team and the rank and file organization: *This is the game we're playing. This is how we're changing the game in our business. This is the kind of culture and human commitment we need to make sure that as we succeed and get bigger we don't lose sight of the fact of those things that made us successful in the first place.*

And there was such a design mindset, not just about what the stores looked like or what their colors were, but also about the business strategy, the expansion strategy, the physical design of the stores, and the social design of the culture. That means that the business became scalable and sustainable.

What strikes me about so many organizations that start fast with a great idea is that eventually they run out of steam because success has a funny way of sowing the seeds of a demise. Can you maintain the same level of urgency and commitment and passion and creativity with 5,000 employees as you did with 50? It's one thing to have some good financial results when the big boys aren't paying any attention to you, but once you get to a size where people are starting to pay attention and the competitive backlash begins, are you able to withstand that competitive backlash?

What impressed me so much about the rise of Commerce Bank to become such a big player is that as it got bigger, the culture remained consistent, the performance remained elevated, and the business strategy continued to hold its own, even as they were going up against some of the biggest banks in the world—and that's another part of the story that really impressed me.

There is such tunnel vision among the big incumbent players in just about every business. It's as if CEO Moses handed down the tablets about "This is what it means to be a bank. This is what it means to be an airline. This is what it means to be a hospital." There's a standard issue strategic mindset. There are all kinds of standard operating procedures and most incumbents are perfectly content to kind of nip and tuck in the margins and, "Hey, we'll be 3 percent cheaper in this product line and we'll try to have our employees be 5 percent more responsive in this service area," and everybody plays the same game. Then you try to be incrementally better than the next guy. Everybody is pretty good at everything.

Then you come across an organization like Commerce that was absolutely the most of something. The most intensely focused on the customer experience; the most intensely focused on gathering deposits as the economic fuel that keeps the engine going. The big established players—and this is not just true of banks, it's true about everything—look at what seems like an alien life force, a kind of outlier to the standard model of the business, and they really don't know what to make of it. They have no capacity to mimic it. It gets bigger and bigger and attracts their attention, so what do they do? They may try to copy a few of the surface innovations. "Okay, we'll stay open a little longer." Or, "We'll put a few coin counting machines in our high-traffic locations." They copy a few of the particular innovations, and yet they don't ever seem to pay any dividends in terms of economic performance because all they're doing is taking on a bunch of the extra costs that a bank like Commerce did, but they're unable to deliver the whole experience so they get none of the benefits.

Vernon told me that the whole point is that it's a *symphony*. The performance works because everything works in concert, so if you don't buy it in its entirety, you can't ever get it to work for you. Vernon's competition over the years simply refused to learn from Commerce.

The classic example of this, outside banking, was in the airline industry where you had the rise of Southwest and JetBlue. Then Delta created Song and United launched Ted. Both tried kind of reluctantly, kind of half-heartedly, to say, "We'll have our version of JetBlue," which was Song for Delta. And "We'll have our version of Southwest," which was Ted for United. And "We'll try to be a little quirky and we'll fly the same 737 plane that Southwest flies and we'll try to turn the planes around in 25 minutes rather than an hour and five minutes." They could never get it to work because they were copying the surface innovations or mimicking the tangible performance, but they didn't have the culture to do it. They didn't have the sense of camaraderie.

Southwest can turn around its planes quickly because everybody works together, including the pilots. If you've got unions that are at odds with one another and unions that are at odds with the company, you can't make all that stuff happen. Two or three years into it United and Delta were completely shocked at how hard it was and they put both Song and Ted out of business. And so it goes in every industry. Incumbent players with an ingrained mindset find it very hard to learn from, let alone mimic, the strategies and practices and culture of a genuine outside-the-box innovator. I see this everywhere, so I'm not that surprised that the big banks (a) never took Commerce seriously, and (b) were never able to figure out how to respond to it because it's outside the established repertoire, basically.

Everybody says "Seeing is believing," but as Steve Jobs said, "Believing is seeing."

15

The New Order: Commercial Banking

I think we are in danger of just becoming the plumbing.

Terry Cordeiro, Head of Digital Transformation, Lloyds Bank,
quoted in *The Drum*, June 17, 2015

Metro Bank also caused a revolution in commercial banking. We are the entrepreneurs' bank in London.

The men and women we recruit to be commercial lenders are good, but the Metro model makes them better because we push them to go out and see their existing customers and introduce themselves to potential new ones.

We want to meet potential new customers and visit their office or store. At any other bank, the employee would probably get the phone slammed down on them. But when someone from our team calls and says, "I'm Geoff from Metro Bank," or we cold call them at their place of business and say, "I'd love to find out a little bit more about your business," they can't help but be curious. Time and again, we find they're inquisitive about Metro because it looks so unlike anything else that's in the city.

We phone lots of commercial businesses (known as cold calling in the United States). All banks tell potential clients that they're genuinely interested in their business. But we'll bring the people that can make a lending decision to the meeting. In the UK, cartel banks won't let the credit guy anywhere near the customer. They avoid it at all costs.

Customers that want to borrow money want to talk to Metro because they already know we're growing and we want more customers. We can't do every deal, but by introducing the potential customer to a decision-maker—sometimes it might even be me or Craig who shows up—they won't have to wait forever for an answer.

It's incredibly powerful because when they see that's how we operate, they will tell their friends, families, and industry counterparts. We help one business owner out, and they tell everyone all about it. That's a Metro differentiator.

We really get inside the business owner's business. If it means we need to meet them three or four times to really understand the business, we'll meet them three or four times. That helps the relationship, long term, because we might structure a loan slightly differently, based on our intimate understanding of their operation. Maybe that's why roughly 70 percent of our business is now commercial, a number that dwarfs what Commerce accomplished.

*

One of our commercial lenders got a tip about a businessman who received credit approval for a multimillion-pound hotel purchase. The bank had worked on the loan for six months. Unfortunately for the customer—but good news for us—the terms were unrecognizable and the commercial lenders at the bank had changed several times during the six months the customer had waited for an answer. It was as if he'd ordered a red sports car and a blue minivan turned up.

Our lender was introduced to the businessman just two weeks before he was due to close the deal on the hotel. He explained that the bank had changed its loan terms at the last minute, assuming he had no choice but to accept.

We knew we didn't have much time. At the first meeting, we sent Mark Price, Metro's Chief Credit Officer, along because at his level, Mark could sign off on a new loan on the spot.

The customer was extremely impressed that we had brought a decision-maker right to his office. They had a really long, detailed meeting. Together, they looked at the hotel, talked about the management team, their aspirations, their background, and, naturally, the specific deal points.

"We know you've got terms already. What do we need to do to win this for you?"

The buyer told us about their original expectation for the loan.

We wanted to help, and Mark proposed structuring a loan so that they paid only interest to start with to ensure they had enough capital for unexpected expenses.

"We can do this," Mark said.

The fly in the ointment was fulfilling the need for due diligence. Unfortunately, in the UK, the local councils that control deeds and other business records are not always as responsive and speedy as might be expected.

Two days later, the lender reported back to the customer that Metro could do the deal, but couldn't guarantee we could complete the due diligence process by the established closing date, now just 12 days away.

"You might want to approach the seller," he said, "and see if they'll delay the close by a week."

The vendor agreed and we completed the entire deal, start to finish, in three weeks. At our end, we alerted our lawyers to clear the decks and be ready to do whatever it took to close the hotel deal. In terms of UK commercial lending speed, we must have set a record.

The best part?

The other bank didn't know what was happening until the date they thought the customer was drawing down the loan. That day they received a stunning call from their former customer to say he had got better terms elsewhere. We gutted them like fish.

But you know what? They had only themselves to blame, because they took six months to approve the loan in the first place, and then changed the rules without prior notice at the last minute.

The hotel buyer and his partners became massive Metro fans.

And after we'd closed the loan, our involvement did not stop. We check in on the buyer every six months or so to see how they're getting on. I've been by the property myself to check it out. They told their friends all about it, opening endless new doors for Metro. They moved all their personal banking business to us as well.

We gave the hotel owners interest-only payments to start with, at a time they bore loads of capital costs. They didn't tell us this straight away, but we knew—because of our experience in the field—what they did not: that whatever you *think* you're buying, you hope it isn't going to go wrong, but it probably *will* in the beginning. Why don't we supply a little bit extra buffer, so if the heating needed fixing, they didn't have to come back to us pleading for an emergency bridge loan.

We told them, "It's much better to have flexibility before you go into it and find out you need to fix the boiler and it's going to cost £150 grand. Coming back to the bank, you're going to feel a bit awkward. We'll cover that *now*."

That attitude made a big difference in winning the deal, because their original bank moved the goal posts so much in the last minutes of regular time. That's not fair; it's not transparent. We'll say, "This is our best offer." Occasionally we'll get into a Dutch auction, but we think there is higher integrity in terms of us saying that was our best offer.

If we competed on rates, it would be a bad proposition. We'll never pay the best rates on deposits. And we'll never give you the lowest lending rate. We'll be competitive. But in return for the borrowing being slightly more expensive, we'll be quicker, we'll be faster, we'll be more flexible, and we'll really understand your business. Smart customers will pay a premium for that because they get to meet the people at Metro who make the lending decisions.

*

We do lose deals on price. That's no secret.

When that happens, we look inward to see if our lender properly described our value-added.

We've got to get it into the customer's head that we are different. If we lose a deal on price, we believe in shaking hands with no hard feelings. "Let's keep in touch," we'll say, "because we know from experience that what you've been offered by our competition may not be the same as you've been promised when their final offer letter arrives in six weeks' time."

A business customer showed us the best loan rate they'd received and we declined to match or better it. "This is not what we're about," we said. So we lost the deal.

Three months later they came back and we offered them the same terms. The second time around, they accepted. We're providing them with exactly what we said we would right at the start: service, service, service.

*

We've done many deals where we do business with a company, and then they bring us into their inner sanctum. There is one customer who's opened quite a few restaurants with our support. And he, in turn, brought us to the attention of scores of other restaurants. Restaurant owners have their own little eco-system in London, their own system of communications and sharing of business information, despite their intense outward rivalries.

Our hours are apparently a great fit for the city's restaurants and pubs; we're open when they open in the morning and need something as simple as change for the day, and we're the last bank to close so that they can deposit the day's receipts much later than anywhere else.

We've picked up a lot of their business because we also welcome them seven days a week. No one else in London offers that convenience. They can even phone their change order ahead, and we'll have their coins and notes ready and prepared, so they can get in and out quickly.

Sometimes the cartel banks send their restaurant customers running into our warm embrace.

Kevin Barrett told me about a coffee shop near our Cheapside store where he buys coffee every morning. He worked the owner for six months to bring his business to Metro.

One day, Kevin jokingly said, "I won't buy any more coffee unless you switch."

That day, the coffee shop owner unloaded his frustration with his current bank, Barclays, which was a 15-minute walk from his location. Every day, he said, he or one of his employees had to spend an hour or so waiting in line at Barclays just to get change to run the business.

"I can't afford to lose a member of my staff for an hour and a half every day," he said in frustration. "And I can't afford to pay him for an hour and a half to stand in line doing nothing but waiting at a bank!"

Kevin promised that would never happen at Metro and the owner switched banks. Today, the coffee shop sends someone over every morning—seven days a week—and their change pack is ready and waiting.

We do a great job because their model is similar to ours. If their service is poor, they're not going to be busy. We're open every day, just like them. We want our customers to leave as fans, happy and satisfied with our service. They get what we're trying to do.

16

Metro Reinvents Private Banking

Chase the vision, not the money; the money will end up following you.

Tony Hsieh, CEO, Zappos

Julie Barnsley, a veteran of the Bank of Scotland, oversees a fascinating piece of Metro Bank business. It includes servicing our 19 foreign embassy clients (including—somewhat ironically for me—the Embassy of the United States), as well as private banking clients, non-profit organizations, and overseas corporations opening local entities in the UK. Her corner of the bank also supports business that comes in from the Metro board of directors and shareholders, as well as business that Craig Donaldson and I bring in personally.

Overseas companies looking to enter the UK find it difficult to get a bank account at any of the other high street banks.

It's a broken process.

But it's a great business for us.

We have four people whose careers rock around the clock: at 8am they might take calls from business customers in Australia; sometimes they're back in at 8pm taking calls from Los Angeles. We entered that business in 2013 and in just two years opened tens of thousands of new business accounts. It's amazing.

As for private banking, that is a piece of business we never developed at Commerce and, frankly, never imagined building at Metro, either. You won't find it in any business plan that Craig or I ever wrote; it developed organically in 2011, another unintended consequence of the bank cartel's disdain for customers in general and Americans in particular.

The timing for us on the private banking side coincided with a lot of the fallout from the 2008 credit crunch, when the bigger banks restructured their private banking offer to cut costs. Year after year ever since, they've offloaded private banking customers who no longer fit their latest and ever increasing investment criteria. Woe to the customer who last year qualified with £1 million in funds under management, and this year is told that the bank can no longer service anyone banking less than £2 million.

And if you no longer qualify, they drop you as a private customer and send you back to their dreary retail network. They're contracting and reducing all the time. High net worth customers are disaffected. They're looking around, asking their friends, "What am I going to do?" And someone will tell them, "Metro Bank does private banking. Go and have a word with them."

The cartel banks don't care if you've banked with them since you were 12, or if your family has been with them for generations. They don't care if you're a movie star, an athlete or a rock star. Nobody cares.

The level of service that we provide through our store network is so far in advance of what these people were getting through the other high street banks that it is almost a private banking service by comparison. Here, our main differential is that they get direct-dial telephone numbers and email addresses that go straight through to a private banking manager. We offer a support team as well.

Want to know a little secret? We lifted part of our private commercial banking team out of HSBC's private bank. These folk were great at what they did but tired of being ordered to mistreat customers they had come to know as friends. They each had specialties, whether it was government and business leaders or entertainers and footballers.

The best part? Private banking already accounts for 20 percent of Metro's balance sheet.

And we're just getting started.

*

We won the commercial banking for the US Embassy when it went out for tender in 2012. We also do the personal banking for American diplomats.

The biggest challenge in inheriting that business was that diplomats and their families know maybe six months in advance that they are coming to London, but there wasn't a system in place for establishing a UK banking presence before they left the US. They had to wait until they arrived in London, and then go to a cartel bank and attempt to survive the process.

We suggested a better approach.

We went to the US Embassy's human resources department and said, "When you're talking to these people in advance of them coming to the UK, ask them if they're interested in having a personal bank account with Metro Bank, and tick that box. By doing that, they give the embassy's HR team in London permission to share personal information with our Metro Bank team."

We opened a full-service store in the basement of the US Embassy. The HR people come there and start the process. We use that as our address confirmation. Housing is pre-designated, so they know in advance where a person/family will be living. We put all the appropriate information into our system and suspend it there until the individual arrives in the UK. On their first day they come to our store with their passport and security pass and we open the account. We can even print cheques, a debit card and a credit card on the spot.

Metro made a decision that if you are in the diplomatic corps for the US government, we expect that you'll be good for an automatic credit limit to use on an overdraft or on a credit card. On day one of arriving in the UK, they have a card ready that enables them to build up a credit footprint and credit score and they have a fully operational current account.

My View
Rohan Silva
Co-founder, Second Home
Maybe you've read about a London-based entrepreneurial start-up engine called Second Home? Co-founded by Rohan Silva, former special adviser to UK Prime Minister David Cameron, it is a business incubator offering shared workplaces to carefully selected and matched new businesses.

I had heard good things about Silva when he was with the government and wanted to kick the tires of his new venture in person.

One of the first things that won me over hit close to home: Silva's wife, Kate McTiernan, is an architect, like my wife, Shirley. Kate designed the offices at Second Home.

Here is what Rohan Silva has to say about his Metro experience.

*

I used to work for Prime Minister David Cameron. A couple of weeks after leaving the government, I had the opportunity to sit down with Vernon Hill and pick his brains on starting a business. He gave me a copy of his book, *FANS Not Customers*.

"Read this book," he said, and I did.

A whole bunch of things we do at Second Home, my company, are taken straight from the book.

The amazing thing about Metro Bank is that whenever you need something, you can drop someone an email, give someone a call, and a human being responds. We live in an age of algorithms and automation. But the ability of two people to get to talk or correspond and deal with a problem quickly is incalculable.

The business team at Metro Bank sat down with us and helped us put together our business plan. They kicked the tires on it. And then they said "Yes." All of it was dealing with humans, not with algorithms. That was powerful. They gave us feedback and said, "Have you thought about doing this?" They added a lot of value.

We'll often be talking to someone at Metro Bank, and they'll say, "We've just been talking to a client of ours. You should connect with them, because they're trying to do something similar." Or "They dealt with the same problem." Or I'll be talking to someone at Metro Bank about how to scale the business, and they'll say, "Talk to our property team. Let me give you a contact name and phone number." They encourage us to leverage the incredible network of the bank and its experiences. It's fantastic! And no one else does it.

Metro's big, stretching ambition is to not just have customers, but to have fans. As an entrepreneur myself, I've got more and more admiration with each passing day for what Vernon and the Metro team have built. I'm constantly encouraging my team to really push themselves to go the extra mile. And that's because of Metro Bank. It is truly "The Entrepreneur's Bank."

Metro Lingo

Successful businesses almost always have unique keywords and phrases that are used internally to describe a culture, or help them build the model. Here we're pulling back the curtain a little further to reveal a few more concepts and programs that make Metro Bank an industry innovator.

AMAZE! Always *exceed* customer expectations; AMAZE is our acronym for five ways to win *FANS not customers.*

AMAZE! Awards A high-energy, large-scale annual awards ceremony to celebrate Metro's star colleagues.

AMAZE! Van The bright blue and red Metro Bank minivans which are painted with Metro's logo on all sides, used to transport Metro Man, and often parked in high visibility areas during special events.

Brand *Who we are, what we are* and *what the customers expect*!

Bump it up Always find a solution to the customers' needs: one to say yes, two to say no.

Buzz/buzzing The excitement generated when Metro Bank colleagues AMAZE! their customers.

Customer That's Customer with a capital "C"—the most important part of our lives at Metro Bank are the people who purchase our products and services because they pay our salaries. *Customers rule!*

Customer experience The *totality* of everything that touches the sense of a customer when he or she comes into contact with Metro Bank—the appearance of a workspace and our colleagues (the way they dress, their tone of voice, their body language), the product presentation, and the overall delivery of service.

FANS What *all* our customers should become by being so satisfied about the AMAZE(ING) service we provide that they talk passionately about Metro as "my bank."

Growth The future of Metro. It's what our investors expect.

Kill all stupid rules The elimination of endless stupid rules.

Magic Fridays The celebration held in all Metro Bank offices every Friday, during which all colleagues wear red business attire (in honor of the color of the Metro logo) to reinforce our brand and energize customers and colleagues.

Magic Money Machine Metro Bank's user-friendly, interactive coin counting machines located in every store, absolutely free to use by customers and non-customers.

Magic shopper A "mystery shopper" visits or contacts our colleagues in order to gauge the company's level of customer service.

Metro Bank culture The *essence* of who we are—the behaviors and beliefs of Metro Bank colleagues that come from an intense dedication to exceeding the expectations of customers.

Metro Man Our official mascot in the shape of the Metro Bank "M" logo. It makes appearances at special events as a symbol of Metro.

Metro Maniacs A group of Metro Bank colleagues, carrying balloons, prizes and other goodies, who make surprise visits to colleagues in recognition of AMAZE(ING) service.

Metro Money Zone Metro Bank's one-of-a-kind financial

education program for kids aged 7–10, parents and teachers, designed to teach the importance of saving, and much more. It includes in-class visits by Metro Bank colleagues, several special events and a wealth of online resources available through **metrobank**online.co.uk/moneyzone

Metropedia An online one-stop knowledge shop where colleagues go to find answers to their Metro Bank questions.

Non-customer Someone who has not taken the opportunity to join the Metro Bank family by opening an account.

One to Say YES, Two to Say NO Our people are trained to say yes, and if they can't say yes, to find somebody who can.

Opportunity What Metro Bank provides for colleagues and investors who want to be part of a rapidly growing company that offers exceptional career advancement and potential for financial growth.

Recognize A virtual recognition scheme in which any colleague can recognize another for providing AMAZE(ING) service. We host monthly events to celebrate these colleagues.

Retailer The mindset that differentiates Metro from all other banks. By thinking like the great power retailers of America (*ie*, McDonald's, Home Depot, Wal-Mart), Metro Bank provides customers with a truly different and better banking experience.

Retailtainment The *art of engaging customers* and creating *moments of magic*.

Satisfaction guarantee cheque To err is human; to recover is Metro. As well as fixing any problems that may arise, we give customers a satisfaction guarantee payment as a token of our sincere apology.

Shareholders Your *boss*, your fellow *colleagues—YOU*!

Ten Minute Principle A Metro Bank policy created to exceed customers' expectations by extending service hours—ten minutes before our stores officially open and ten minutes after we officially close.

Warm transfer Customer calls that need to be directed to another Metro Bank team member are processed by waiting for the next person to answer the phone, explaining the customer's situation in full, and providing the customer with the new team member's name before putting the transfer through.

17

The Disruptor: "What Will You Do Next?"

To be a benevolent organization, you have to make a lot of profit. But if your sole goal is to maximize profit, you're on a collision course with time. We've made commitments that have become accretive to the brand, but it was never by design.

Howard Schultz, chairman, Starbucks

My father, who sold his real estate business and retired in 1992, was proud of my success with Commerce Bank.

When he died a few years later, the bank had assets of $4 billion. To him, it was a tremendous success. But his attitude was, "Well, that's over with, what will you do next?" And rather than be insulted by that as some might be, I felt the same way. We have a company line: "We got paid for last year's success already, what are we doing now?"

*

When we're talking about entrepreneurs that are successful, what are some of the common traits? They have informed instinct. They shape the world around them; they don't let the world shape them. Think, for instance, about Harry Gordon

Selfridge, Charles Dunstone, Steve Jobs, or Sam Walton: they all defied and disrupted the conventional wisdom of their era. They ignored what everybody said and shaped the world around their ideas.

We would never have come to London if the model had not proven itself in New York.

We no longer go through as many hoops to get people to know who we are and what we stand for in London. Instead, the more common question has become, "When are you coming to *my* neighborhood?" Word-of-mouth advertising works spectacularly well when your focus is on creating fans, not customers.

It's also fundamentally easier to find colleagues that want to work with us, for the same reasons.

It's been proved; Metro Bank works in London, even better than Commerce ever did in New York.

When Americans moving here ask me what it's like, I say, "The people are magnificent, intelligent, personable and have a sense of humor that takes some getting used to. London itself is absolutely stunning, from the River Thames vistas to the architecture found at Parliament and modern designs such as The Shard. Be careful in traffic, though: it's every man, woman and child for themselves. And the food will surprise you; burgers, fries and pizza as good as home, plus every variation on international and gourmet cuisine your heart desires."

*

The British media refer to Metro Bank and the newer banks that have followed us onto London's high street as "challenger" banks, theorizing that we are challenging the Old Guard to move their staid practices into the modern era.

But I think of our approach as that of a *disruptor*. We're shaking and reshaping the city's perceptions of what a bank is and what interacting with one should be like.

The market is excited about our disruptor model and the award-winning technology we introduced.

The British banks treat their commercial customers even worse than their personal customers. Opening a new business account takes 6–8 weeks. We will open one the same day.

Having said that, Brits are slow to switch banks, supermarkets, lawyers, doctors—you name it. They also have an ingrained belief that if something is good, it must be too good to be true. The switching process is a little harder in Britain, as there's no tradition of bank switching. The fact that we've got the numbers we have—despite all that—is remarkable. It points out how desperate so many people are to be treated better.

Metro worked as a disruptor by ignoring the conventional British way of doing things and, instead, doing the right thing for the British public.

All I've done is remind them of what they're missing. It's difficult to describe how much people hate the cartel banks. We just brought their hate and disgust to the forefront.

This was not just opening another new bank, as we did with Commerce in Manhattan in 2001. We're years ahead of the British banking establishment in every way. It's like we're from Mars. They know it, the media know it, the government knows it, and the customer knows it. We've set up a revolutionary model in Britain, and it's been accepted.

Everything we did in America works better in Britain because there hasn't been anything new in British high street banking for 100-plus years.

*

On 7 March 2016, Metro Bank launched its long anticipated initial public offering (IPO).

We needed to raise capital to support rampant growth and the time was right. I promised the original Metro investors that we'd go public in about five years. In Britain, particularly, the markets see it as a coming of age, a validation.

The stores massively over-performed against what we originally predicted.

I came over, invested £20 million of my own money, took a gamble, and after five-plus years the company was listed on the main London exchange, with a market value of £1.6 billion ($2.4 billion) on opening day. We created that value from scratch. That's good in America, but it's almost beyond their comprehension in London.

Going public is about raising capital to support the bank. It's about making our stock marketable, it's about making our options work, and it's about raising our visibility.

It is a recognition of Metro's success.

*

Why do we get so much good press? Service, innovation, and one more important factor: none of the big banks will talk to the financial press in London because they know they're going to get a bad story. So for any story about banking, the reporters come to us. And in a metropolitan area with 10 daily newspapers, that's a lot of press for the competition to hide from.

Reporters hate the banks. And they use us as a weapon to beat up on the cartel.

After being skeptical of us for the first year, we went through, "Oh, you guys are doing what you said you would do. It's not a fake!" And then they became supporters. Somebody will take a shot at us occasionally. They'll say we're not making money yet. But generally the press have been great to Metro.

*

Metro Bank founding CEO Craig Donaldson and I are very different, but alike, which is why the relationship works.

As I write this, Craig is 43 years old. I am 27 years his senior but we've already worked together for nearly seven years. It's been quite a journey and I believe we learn from each other every day. He and I are similar in that we both love banking. We both want to build something of which we're proud, and leave a legacy. And we both want to do the right thing by our colleagues and our customers.

"Behind closed doors, Vernon and I can have a bloody good discussion," Craig said. "We can't do it in front of people, but we can behind closed doors. And as long as I have the conviction of my beliefs and I have numbers to back them up, Vernon listens. On a couple of occasions, I've gone into Vernon and said, 'I can't prove this, Vernon, but I really believe this. This is what I think we should do.' And he backed it. That comes with time and trust. You've got to be willing to back yourself, if you're going to build something. We can have agreements and disagreements, but Vernon listens. That's often missed about him in the press."

*

An old British banking adage is: "Service and convenience are charming when you are small, but when you get bigger, you can't do it."

I think we proved the cartel was wrong about that!

Size breeds momentum! But it can also breed complacency. This model of ours is about getting into people's heads, hearts, minds, and souls, and then letting them do their jobs. We don't micromanage. Our environment, our culture, and our management style are not about that. We worried about bringing in veterans of Britain's antiquated banking culture: would their bad old habits seep through and ruin our culture? Fortunately, that has not happened. In addition to de-programming new people joining us, we AMAZEd them into seeing that ours really is a better way.

Great businesses create fans by redefining or creating industries through unique combinations of the model + culture + execution formula. By creating great brands they then create value, which benefits everyone from the fans to the shareholders.

Anyone who has created a true growth company—whether it's Bill Gates with Microsoft, Ray Kroc with McDonald's, or Warren Buffett with Berkshire Hathaway—has been an agent of change by creating a new industry; reinventing an existing industry; going against conventional wisdom; enduring the barbs of the competition, media, and a skeptical public; and thinking outside the box.

During the early days of Metro Bank's opening in London, we were attacked and opposed by the British banking cartel, business reporters, and skeptics. For most, we were too small to matter and they assumed we wouldn't grow enough to warrant much attention. As for the competition, they convinced themselves that a service-focused model would never work in London. Soon, they said we were only getting the accounts nobody wanted!

Today, it's a little harder for them to explain away the 1,000 new accounts we open every day.

But I have a simple explanation: we create *FANS not customers* and those fans love talking about us!

*

My job at Metro Bank is to protect the brand, to define the brand, and to expand the brand. And to that end, I have five basic responsibilities every day of my working life:

- **Develop** the model
- **Install** the model

- **Instill** the model
- **Enforce** the model
- **Improve** the model

Every entrepreneur has the same responsibility.

Our business model is to attack the competition, their stupid rules and wrong-headed traditions—attack on the ground, attack in the air, attack in the media.

We have a saying at Metro Bank: "To err is human; to recover is Metro." We will make errors, whether at Metro Bank or Petplan, but how we recover from those errors will determine whether you are a fan, not a customer.

Our people are told, "We only have a few rules, but you are empowered to overrule them."

That's the opposite of the message that every other bank employee gets at every other bank.

We're not perfect; we do make mistakes. But our model and culture call for us to own up to our errors, make corrections and recover as fast as possible, and leave no unhappy customers in our wake.

Recovery takes many forms:

- **Step 1: Take ownership of the problem**
- **Step 2: Listen to find the problem**
- **Step 3: Clarify and clearly understand the problem, and repeat it back to the customer**
- **Step 4: Solve the customer's problem**
- **Step 5: The satisfaction guarantee**

If we can't correct the issue, we will attack the result. If a customer's cheque bounces, we will endeavor to help them deal with it.

There is an art to recovery. For us, every problem is an opportunity to win over a customer and hopefully create a new fan. We won't ostracize or fire colleagues for making an error. Most mistakes can be fixed, and we tell colleagues that. We tell them, "If you make a mistake, alert us immediately so we can make it right."

We take ownership of every customer's problem—and solve it. The buck stops with our team member. If they can't solve the basic problem, they will take care of any inconveniences it causes. Then they help us deliver AMAZE!ing service by asking a manager or supervisor for a satisfaction guarantee cheque that they can present to the customer who encountered the snag.

We want our customers to know we're dedicated to providing them with AMAZE!ing service at all times.

*

My career journey has gone beyond my expectations. Metro Bank is another example of a concept I first created in 1973. Our fans took us to unimagined success. The value-differentiated Metro Bank model, and our pervasive culture and unique execution, continually create fans.

Remember this: if we can change retail banking in Britain, there isn't anything *you* can't change in your business!

The best is yet to come at Metro Bank and I wish you good luck in *your* own revolutionary enterprise!

*

PS: Have you applied the *Fans not customers* model to your business? Tell us about it for consideration in a future edition. Send your business story to FANS@metrobank.plc.uk

Appendices

Appendix 1

Petplan: Insurance for Our Four-Legged Friends

> The most important thing in life is to stop saying I wish and to start saying I will. Consider nothing impossible, then treat possibilities as probabilities.
>
> Charles Dickens, author, *David Copperfield*

The Metro Bank story is one of offering major value, achieved by creating a differentiated model infused with a unique culture and delivered with fanatical execution.

What if I told you that we also applied *FANS not customers* to a completely different industry, one previously held in such low esteem it made bankers look good?

Bernie Marcus and Arthur Blank reinvented home improvement retailing. Steve Jobs did the same for computer, mobile phone and tablet sales. IKEA did it for low-cost, high-quality furniture. If we can do it for retail banking, what's stopping *you* from reinventing *your* business?

Petplan is another great example of our philosophy and execution at work. Two British entrepreneurs fulfilled their American dream by creating a new model for pet health insurance in the US by applying the New Maths.

Chris and Natasha Ashton have created *FANS not customers*

at America's third largest pet health insurer by redefining the business and creating a new model and major wealth.

Although hugely popular and successful in the UK, the pet insurance industry struggled mightily in the US market. The American company that pioneered the industry back in the 1970s had modeled itself on a human health model that, as we all know, is seriously broken. As a result, it created products that didn't provide value or allow the industry to gain in purpose, stature, or economic surety. And its reputation for being customer-friendly was frightfully bad.

This presented someone, somewhere, with the opportunity to succeed and change the course of an entire industry, if only they had access to the right model, culture and execution—someone like Chris and Natasha Ashton.

*

America's love affair with pets becomes more extreme by the day. Pets are the new American kids! We look at pets very differently now than we did even ten years ago. If it costs $8,000 to keep your dog alive and thriving, many families will choose to spend the money. And veterinary practice has reached the point where it's almost equal to human practice and cost.

Pet insurance was invented in the UK. And Petplan UK, which opened its doors in the mid-1970s, is the largest pet health insurer in the world. One-third of pets in Britain have health insurance; in America, less than 1 percent of our 175 million dogs and cats are so protected.

In Philadelphia, Pennsylvania, we created Petplan, a tremendous, fast-growing, top-rated company that will protect our customers' beloved pets and create great wealth and opportunity for our colleagues and shareholders.

The story of Petplan in the US started, as many new businesses do, with an unexpected crisis. It became a true American success story.

Chris and Natasha Ashton were MBA candidates at my alma mater, Wharton School of Business at the University of Pennsylvania. They moved to Philadelphia in 2001 from their native Britain with four suitcases and a Birman cat named Bodey. Barely a month into their studies, the cat became quite ill.

Five thousand dollars in veterinary expenses later, they started looking into pet insurance and were distressed by the extremely limited choices compared with what they had in the UK. A family emergency blossomed into their passion.

The Ashtons, who met at Oxford University, came to Wharton to further explore an entrepreneurial career, one that leveraged Chris's military security experience after seven years as a Royal Marine Commando and Natasha's background in shipping.

But as they painfully paid that vet bill and moved into less costly living quarters to cut expenses, the Ashtons had a fresh moment of inspiration: Americans needed a new and improved model if pet insurance was to ever catch fire in the US.

"We thought we could leverage our knowledge of pet insurance in the UK and introduce a product that provides a type of coverage that the American market hadn't seen before," Natasha said. "We wanted to reinvent and redefine American pet insurance."

It quickly became apparent that it was an enormous business opportunity, even during the economic downturn then gripping the country. Pet products, it turns out, are generally recession-proof.

It was a great idea, but they had no capital to start a national business in an unfamiliar land—indebted as they already were thanks to $250,000 in student loan debt.

The Ashtons quickly realized that Americans' pet obsession runs just as deep as—*or deeper than*—that of Europeans when they saw that pets are a bigger industry than toys or candy. (In 2015 alone, Americans were projected to spend more than $60 billion on their pets, according to the American Pet Products

Association. Per head, Americans spend more on pets than folks do in Europe.)

The Ashtons refined a business plan that for the first time provided real value to American pet owners. They learned that, according to Datamonitor (2008), one in every three pets requires unexpected veterinary care each year. In addition, 40 percent of all claims received by Petplan are for chronic conditions that last beyond 12 months. These statistics show that health insurance for pets has become a financial necessity, not a luxury. Dramatic advances in veterinary medicines have provided pet owners with new treatment options, but these can be expensive. In 2009–10, American pet owners spent $12.2 billion on veterinary care, and that number is expected to rise.

Pet insurance can be an invaluable tool for pet owners as it allows for the best care, but it also prevents them from having to make difficult decisions regarding their pets' health. The financial burden that pet owners may face should a beloved pet become seriously ill or injured can be alleviated through insurance, which can help provide life-saving treatment. Ultimately, pet insurance is a smart way for pet owners to be forward thinking in protecting the health of these beloved family members and perhaps, more importantly, preserve their own peace of mind by minimizing the financial burden that can come from unexpected health crises.

Consider this: there are more than 500 inherited diseases in purebred dogs and more than 300 in mixed-breed dogs. At the time of the Ashtons' inquiry, no American pet insurer was providing coverage for those kinds of treatment. And yet those were precisely the costs people were looking to protect themselves against. Under existing American pet policies, the Ashtons would have been reimbursed just $500 on their cat's $5,000 vet bill, which didn't make any sense.

Petplan UK, the world's largest pet insurance provider, based just outside London, granted the Ashtons an exclusive license in the US and gave them access to 30 years' worth of proprietary actuarial pet data, experience, and know-how, which enabled them to create the products that were revolutionary in the marketplace.

They sold their first policy in July 2006. Two years later, Petplan was licensed in all 50 states.

In its first five years of operation, in one of the most challenging economic climates the world had seen in a long time, Petplan experienced tremendous growth, rising to number 123 in *Inc.* magazine's list of the 500 Fastest Growing Companies in America in 2011.

For a premium of $300–400 per year, customers receive an annual coverage limit of $10,000–20,000 a year and the pet is covered for life.

Petplan now has more than 150,000 pets insured in the US and, while that is an enormous number for a start-up—as is the 30 percent annual growth rate—it's just a fraction of the uninsured dogs and cats across the nation. There is a phenomenal need and opportunity to act. When the Ashtons have insured just 1 percent of the pets in America, the value of the company will be $1 billion.

*

Petplan is an example of building a serious new company from scratch by actually exceeding the New Maths described in Chapter 5:

Model + Culture + Execution = Fans

Protect the brand (do nothing stupid!)

Refine the brand (make it better all the time!)

Expand the brand (find new products and
new areas where we can add value!)

At Petplan, there are many things that set us apart from our competitors. First and foremost is our approach to the business as a whole. We conceived this company as a pet health business first and foremost and secondarily as an insurance company. This approach really underpins everything we do because we are strictly focused on pet health. Pets come first, and this led us to create policies that are far more comprehensive than any competitor's.

We provide simple, straightforward policies with no exclusions, relatively speaking.

Being a pet company, not an insurance company, is a real distinction for us and it helps to create *FANS not customers* because no one enjoys buying insurance. We're more focused on being pet people and being a pet company. That's how we create the passion that is essential to build our brand.

Our model is that of a premium service, not a cheap, low-value product.

Chris and Natasha started Petplan with an engaging, clearly defined brand that set it apart from the competition. I later challenged them to aggressively pursue partnerships and to open up more channels on a nationwide and international basis. We expanded into Canada, and that was only the beginning.

Instead of an acquisition and merger approach, the Ashtons have built from the ground up in Canada, putting in place a strong dog breeder program so that we are introduced to new pet owners at the moment of adoption. They partnered with Best Friends, a chain of boarding kennels and vet clinics.

Partnerships have helped grow the business. AARP (an acronym for the American Association of Retired Persons) has 38 million members and is the largest partner that they've signed.

Six months after graduating from Wharton, Chris heard about a business plan competition being held at the school that was aimed at baby boomers. It was the first time the Ashtons had thought about this growing market segment's potential for future pet insurance policies.

Although they didn't win, one of the judges was from AARP. "She pulled us aside," Natasha recalls, "and said, 'This is a fantastic idea. Our members absolutely need this, and we should talk.'"

But Petplan had not yet launched and AARP was wary of going into business with a company that existed only on paper. They said, "Go off and start your business, and come back."

Every few years, the Ashtons went back. But for a long time, AARP wasn't ready.

A few years ago, I heard that AARP did a survey and found that their members were extremely interested in pet insurance. They put out a request for proposals (RFP) for pet insurance and we officially threw our hat in the ring. In 2014, Petplan was named the official pet insurance company of AARP, giving us access to their 38 million members.

Ironically, being named the official pet insurance company of AARP gave an enormous credibility boost to the entire pet insurance industry for the first time.

Another area where we've seen a lot of growth is aligning with the blues—the Blue Cross/Blue Shield companies. We're working with eight of them now, with more in the pipeline. This involves a lot of work, because even though they all come under the Blue Cross/Blue Shield umbrella, they're all independent companies, and they make their own decisions based on their own priorities. For many, pet insurance isn't a priority yet, but they've all seen the benefits of it. Margins on human health insurance declined under Obamacare, so they're looking for ancillary products.

They're interested in creating an additional touch point with their existing customers. They're giving something of value, protecting another family member to go with their human coverage.

The Ashtons also identified employee benefits programs

as having vast market potential. Many large companies offer insurance as an employee benefit. We've signed deals with Lego, Warner Brothers, SpaceX, and NASCAR, to name a few.

*

When I joined Petplan as chairman, the company was only open from 9 to 5, five days a week. I said to Chris and Natasha, "That's ridiculous. First, why aren't you open later during the week, and second, why aren't you open on Saturdays and Sundays? Our banks are open seven days a week. Don't pet families want the same convenience and flexibility?" We extended our opening hours, making assistance available earlier and later than any other pet insurance company.

We think of Petplan not as a pet insurance company but as a pet health company that happens to sell insurance. Our marketing is geared around selling, yet also educating. Our primary sales challenge is educating people to get them comfortable enough to want to buy.

It comes down to service. We're a service company, whether that service is banking or pet health. When people call Petplan, they are often emotional, they're upset, their pet is sick and it's like a family member is ill. They need to talk to someone who will be empathetic, not hiding behind a website interface.

*

Petplan's success is aided by the nature of its main competitor, which has a complicated policy and schedule of benefits. Claimants are paid so much for this, so much for that, and the insurer spends its waking hours fighting *not* to pay valid claims. Many vets and customers dislike it immensely. At Petplan, customers submit their vet bill, we review it, subtract a deductible, and pay the balance.

Our main competitor does not cover hereditary diseases. But at least half of pet health problems today are hereditary diseases! Every breed has them, even mixed breeds.

And finally, most other companies won't accept pets as new enrollments after a certain age—typically 8–10 years old—the age at which most pets, like people, begin to break down.

All of these are anti-customer gimmicks. We do just the opposite. We kill every stupid rule so there's a clear differentiation between what we offer as a product, brand, and service levels—*model + culture + execution = FANS not customers*—and what the competition sells.

*

I met the Ashtons through our family's involvement at the University of Pennsylvania's School of Veterinary Medicine. I bought into their vision and came on board as chairman in 2008, making a serious investment in the company.

Shirley and I liked the idea of working with an up-and-coming, husband-and-wife management team. We saw a lot of ourselves in Chris and Natasha—not to mention our shared love of pets. A business mentoring relationship developed quite naturally, and we're proud of our association with Petplan and its adoption of many Metro Bank principles.

Natasha runs the marketing of the business. Chris focuses on business development, deals and partnerships. In everything else, they work jointly.

Overall, they provide each other with a trusted, reliable pair of clear eyes and fresh thinking.

"So much of what we do here," Chris said, "Wharton doesn't teach you. Microeconomics is great, but it's not helpful on a day-to-day basis. You want to create a simulation? Fantastic! But that doesn't help you sell or manage colleagues or attract business partners. What Wharton taught us was how to work hard. And it opened us up to an extraordinary network. It educated us to know that if there's an area in which we're not sure of the answers, we know where to look for the appropriate resources to be sure. It taught us how to think and not to panic."

"There is always a solution," adds Natasha. "There is always a way. If you get enough talented people to work alongside you, you'll find a way. Sometimes it's not as simple as you'd like, but there's always a way."

Chris and Natasha began refining their business model by adopting many of our proven business principles. Petplan is succeeding by focusing on the *FANS not customers* New Maths:

- **Differentiated model.** By insuring hereditary diseases, paying vet bills without a claims schedule, and focusing on pets, not insurance, the company reinvented and redefined the market.
- **Unique culture.** With Petplan's institutionalized love of pets and a total service culture, the company reinforces its model.
- **Fanatical execution.** We get happy customers, 100 percent of the time—and a remarkable 80-plus percent renewal rate.

The result is *FANS not customers*:

- More than 10 percent market share, number three American pet insurer
- 50 percent compound growth rate
- 80 percent policy renewals.

*

One of the other things I've tried to instill in the Ashtons is that they have to be visible spokespersons for their brand—the "Pied Pipers" of Petplan.

"That was a bit alien to us, but now we see it," Chris said. "It's essential that the business has a personality behind it, and here, that's the two of us."

They learned the secrets of American-style business networking, constantly telling their company's story to everyone they met.

Another area of emphasis on which I have worked with the Ashtons is speed of decision-making. When we met, they over-analyzed everything, often to the point of business paralysis. They like to not make mistakes, but in business, you've got to make a decision and confidently move ahead. Nobody knows every time which decisions will work and which won't. But you'll never know if you don't choose.

"If anything, we learned that inaction will kill the business," Natasha said. "You'd be better off making the decision and correcting all the way than just doing nothing."

*

One of the first things that the Ashtons and I agreed upon in joining forces on Petplan was that to build a culture, we must hire for attitude and train for skill. If we hire people who are passionate about pets and who empathize with our policyholders, that practice will set us up for the best types of experiences.

It's much easier to find passionate pet people and teach them insurance than it is to find people who have an insurance background and teach them to be passionate about pets. It just doesn't work. Petplan hires people who are pet mad, and helps them through the licensing.

Recruiting is a behavior. We can teach technical skills, but our culture, when it focuses on customer services, is the ability to be *nice*—the ability to smile all the time, to exceed expectations.

The lion's share of these things is innate, and that's what our culture is built around because it's our differentiator. Knowing, understanding, and matching our culture to our business model, and hiring the right people and training them the right way is the key to success in any business. We may just believe in it more strongly than other companies.

Just as important to maintaining a great culture is recognizing when we make a mistake by hiring someone who doesn't absorb and apply our unique culture. If a person doesn't fit within our culture, and cannot execute our model, perhaps Petplan is not the right place for them.

*

At Petplan, the *FANS not customers* approach underpins everything we do.

It's not just a question of meeting customers' expectations. Every day, we look for ways to go above and beyond, from planting a tree in memory of their dog or cat when it passes away to hand-delivering policies if we need to support a customer in an extraordinary situation.

Everyone in the company will go out of their way to make sure that our policyholders continue receiving the kind of service and support that will make them tell their family and friends about us.

At Petplan, our customer call center is often the company's primary contact with policyholders. This is where we build and earn *FANS not customers*.

We have a three-week training program in place, but every person we hire *must* be passionate about pets, must be a pet lover first and foremost, because otherwise they couldn't possibly begin to empathize with the owner of a sick or injured dog or cat.

We ask them, "Do you have pets?," and we can tell immediately what kind of pet owner they are. We talk about their pets and how they feel about their pets and what kind of experience they've had when their pets are sick. We ask, "How did that make you feel?," and "How was your experience with the veterinarian?" That's how we determine whether they're going to be able to guide our policyholders through traumatic events when their pets are sick.

Most of a policyholder's experience with the Petplan call center happens off script because we want our colleagues to empathize with the policyholder. It's more of a question of having tools that they can use. When someone calls up and says they have a Cavalier King Charles spaniel, our people can immediately say, "Oh, our founders have one of those! They're great dogs, very affectionate, but did you know they suffer from congenital heart conditions?"

Our happiness managers on the service side form deep bonds with policyholders. In one case, a manager learned that a Petplan policyholder was going through cancer treatment at the same time as her dog. She called up fairly regularly as she struggled to deal with her own illness and her pet's at the same time. The same manager always took the woman's call, always spent as much time as needed to console the customer, comfort her, and one day she even sent her a big bouquet of flowers.

Petplan serves a never-ending stream of unique dog and cat owners, such as the woman who just adopted two new puppies.

"I remember answering the call," Natasha said, "and she was whispering. I couldn't understand why she was whispering. It turned out that she had the dogs in the car with her and she didn't want the one dog to overhear. She was heading back to the breeder to return the one puppy. She said, 'I don't want to hurt his feelings, but he's a little bit aggressive.' She wanted to see if it was okay if she returned him. Would the other puppy still be insured?" (Yes.)

Early on, Petplan adopted the *FANS not customers* approach of "One to say yes, two to say no." When we have to tell somebody no, how do we make sure it's the right decision? We instituted a steadfast policy that before a team member says no to a customer for any reason, they must check with somebody else.

In the call center, if a customer service representative (CSR) is on the verge of denying a claim, they are instructed to tell a policyholder, "Let me check on this one more time for you. Do you mind if I put you on hold for a second?" Then they'll reach out to a supervisor and say, "I have a denial pending. I want to make sure I'm telling them the right thing. Can you review this?"

We train our Petplan CSRs that they are there for the customer *first*. They are there for the company *second*:

"When you take the call, be the advocate for the customer," Natasha said. "Listen intently. Listen with empathy. Listen to what their issue is before you make a judgment, before you rush to decide. Get all the facts. At that point you can speak on behalf of the company. But while you're listening, while you're engaging with that customer, that's all you should care about."

We try to do the same thing in claims. We understand that a policyholder's claim is not just a form to them. It's not just an invoice or a medical record. On the other side of that claim is a pet, a member of their family.

We must never forget that there are four furry paws at the end of everything we do—that every policy sold, claim processed, and health article published has a real effect on a pet's quality of life. Our model and vision is to put pets first:

- A dog ingested some cocaine and PCP (also known as angel dust), and we paid about $20,000 for that. I had a laugh afterwards thinking, "How did your pet get these narcotics?" I was happy that we were able to help her, but I had so many questions. It was an accident, and we pay for all accidents that aren't pre-existing.
- We had an unrelated claim for a dog that picked up some

crack on a walk. We're not sure how the owners knew it was crack.

- A two-year-old Great Dane started sneezing, and he was consistently experiencing a bloody nose over six days. The vet couldn't figure it out. The medical record said, repeatedly, "Dog's making a weird face." Eventually, they went to a specialist. The Dane was sedated. They did a rhinoscopy and found a 6-inch wooden corndog skewer in his nose. ($5,000)

Our supervisors audit all claims over $10,000. Those are generally the more interesting stories that we see. A cat was hanging out of the window of a New York City high-rise, and decided to take a leap. It fell nine stories. It fractured almost everything—hind limbs, forelimbs. Its back was broken in a few places. Its hips were broken. It was completely mangled, this poor cat. But it survived the fall. ($20,000)

More wild stories:

- A young mastiff had severe bone deformities in her back legs, her femurs in particular. They were so malformed that the surgeons were afraid to go in and make the cuts in her bone to try to orient them appropriately; they weren't sure it would work because they were so unusually shaped. We paid for an MRI scan, and a one-quarter/one-half scale model of the dog's femurs from a 3D printer ($5,000). The surgeons made the cuts on the practice femur to see if they would be viable and hold together, before they did surgery on the dog itself.

- A cat owner brought an interesting "foreign body" claim. The cat had only been under policy for about a month, and he ate some string that became lodged in his intestines. This kitty was really sick. He had every post-op complication you could have. He was severely septic. His bowels had perforated due to the severity of the foreign body. A large section of his intestines were removed. We paid for feeding tubes and extensive ICU critical care hospitalization. He hadn't eaten for so long that he suffered esophageal stricture (narrowing of the esophagus). The vet inserted stents to help inflate his esophagus so that food could pass through again. ($22,000)

- A dog went in for a regular check-up and the owner said that he was a little bit off, so she asked if the vet would do a cancer screen. They found a tumor at the base of the brain stem. ($15,000)

- In Canada, paying for treatment after a moose attacks a dog is becoming more common.

- We get frequent claims for treatment after a dog eats a light bulb.

And if there is a complication in a dog's pregnancy and she needs to deliver via C-section, we will pay for that.

In addition to traditional veterinarian treatments, we pay for holistic and alternative medicine including acupuncture, herbal supplements, chiropractic, raindrop therapy, therapeutic massage, and oxygen treatment. If the policyholder's vet is recommending it, or thinks it works, it's not really our place to tell the vet no. (Although sometimes we will research the practitioner to be sure of their bona fides.)

We decline elective care (docking tails, cracking ears for appearances, spaying/neutering) and we don't pay for routine annual care. Someone wanted a flashlight for their cat's collar because it was going blind. *No.* Laser machine to administer in-home treatment? *No.* Cosmetic dentistry for show dogs? *No.* Stem cells? *Yes.* Cloning? *No.*

(Our customer call center reps can't help but make some unusual faces while taking calls. Laughing is frowned upon, naturally.)

We're always looking for ways to connect; these really are

genuine relationships. You can ask any of our happiness managers—a lot of them will refer to policyholders as friends.

We came to realize fairly early on that by virtue of the nature of our business, all the pets we insure will at some point pass away, and we lose many pets over the policy year. A company we support will plant a tree in the pet's name and then send a note to the policyholder to let them know that we've commemorated their family's loss.

Couple those relationships with all the things that we do very, very well—cash management, extended hours, no stupid rules—and we wind up with *FANS not customers* across all our business lines.

*

Marketing is an area in which that couldn't possibly be truer.

"Design is a competitive advantage and we have really focused on the design of everything that Petplan does," Chris said, "from the office itself all the way through collateral marketing materials such as our magazine and website. Everything we do is highly designed. We rely on photography to reach out and touch people and that has really worked in our favor. It's something that Commerce Bank was about from the get-go."

Petplan doesn't have stores like Metro Bank does. But that's *precisely* why design is a competitive weapon in its business as well. Because pet insurance is an intangible product, design is paramount. We focused on creating a pet-friendly brand, and design underpins everything we do.

The product that a customer buys from us is a policy. And most pet insurance policies are black-and-white, 8.5 × 11 inch pieces of paper with just the details printed on them because that's the easiest way to do it. Our marketing team designed beautiful policy documents that are now sent electronically—saving printing and shipping costs—with color throughout. Pet families don't expect this in their first interaction with us. These well-crafted documents tie in with the Petplan website (www. gopetplan.com) and also our call center.

Our Petplan offices are also beautifully designed because they are part of the culture, part of our brand. The offices don't resemble those of a typical insurance company. There are bright yellow walls with dog bowls hanging on them. There's amazing photography of America's beloved pets everywhere you walk. From the beginning we felt that photography would engage our potential customers, so we recruited the services of one of the country's leading pet photographers, Amanda Jones. She has taken thousands of photos of our policyholders' pets which we then use across our marketing materials.

"We want our headquarters to be a happy place. That's really important to us," Natasha said. "We want our colleagues to be able to communicate joy to our policyholders. In order to do that, the environment has to reflect it, which is why I picked yellow. Yellow is a happy color. And there are pets everywhere. The space speaks the brand, which has evolved as slightly quirky, but fun."

We introduced the first-ever pet health magazine, *fetch!*, distributed free to all our policyholders.

When we first launched *fetch!*, there was a significant start-up cost. It's not a cheap publication, certainly when you consider the element of design and the high quality of the paper that we use. Early on it cost us more to produce than pretty much anything else, but we couldn't put a price tag on what it did for our relationship with policyholders and our renewal rates. Now the magazine pays for itself through advertising, but right from the start, I didn't object to spending the money because it's about long-term relationship building.

Sometimes, if you're focused so much on cost, you miss the bigger picture.

fetch! has become so popular that it now has a paid subscriber base. It is sold nationwide through Barnes & Noble and continues to gain in popularity. It's one of the most widely read pet publications in America.

We also created a pet health blog. Our website is focused on animal health, so from policy design all the way to our interaction with the consumer, everything we do focuses on pet health as opposed to just the transaction of insurance.

Through this attention to design—on top of our customer-centric service and commitment to pet owners—we have made our mark on the industry and clearly differentiated Petplan from the competition. Every touch point with the customer is beautiful to behold. The website is clean, it's easy to use.

Petplan has a strong social media presence on Facebook, Pinterest, Twitter and Instagram. Pinterest routinely uses Petplan as a poster child for how to leverage Pinterest as a vehicle in a business setting. They even wrote a case study on Petplan.

There is often a disconnection between how our customers view us and how we view our service. A perfect answer was when we rolled out our live chat customer service feature. We never imagined how powerful that would be. It rapidly became our second highest channel of choice for our customers.

Another channel between Petplan and the marketplace is the Petplan Veterinary Awards, like Metro Bank's AMAZE Awards. Started in 2012 to honor Petplan's veterinary community, the awards include:

- Practice of the Year
- Veterinarian of the Year
- Veterinary Technician of the Year
- Practice Manager of the Year
- Receptionist of the Year
- Pet Parent of the Year

The black-tie gala is held in Orlando, Florida, in conjunction with the North American Veterinary Conference and co-sponsored by the Animal Hospital Association, the American Veterinary Medical Association and National Vet Tech Association, making it the leading awards ceremony for the industry.

Whether you're walking into the Petplan office, reading *fetch!*, picking up one of our brochures, surfing the website, discovering the company via social media, winning a professional recognition awards from us, or receiving our newsletter, you know it's Petplan. You can't miss the quality.

*

Petplan has been another great example of creating wealth by adding customer value through a unique, differentiated model, a persuasive culture supporting the model, and the right financial execution.

In the same way that I tell people not to compare Metro to other banks, but to retail stores, the Ashtons prefer being compared to a company such as Uber rather than another insurance company.

Using the Uber smartphone app to order a ride is the easiest thing in the world. It's seamless and beautifully designed, and the customer experience is great. Uber removed friction between it and the customer at every step, and that's what Petplan is trying to do.

(*Forbes* magazine, incidentally, named Petplan one of its "Most Promising Companies" for three years in a row.)

We align the Petplan strategy and structure to follow customer experience and ensure that it's a good one. As companies grow, they tend to develop a silo approach. This department, that department, and how do we interact between them? The Ashtons' approach is to tie everything together: "Let's have a web of customer experiences and we'll put our stamp on every piece of it." Whenever something affects the customer, you'll find somebody on the Petplan team making sure it's a good experience.

Just like at Metro, at Petplan it's all about empowering the team, allowing frontline people to make decisions. Chris and Natasha help structure those decisions and protect the rest of the company experience. But they allow their people to make decisions. This approach breeds an environment where, instead of people just passing along problems, they come with solutions. Instead of management saying, "That's what the policy is" or "That's the way the system is built," Petplan's leadership culture responds: "What do you think would be right? What would you suggest if this were your company? How would you handle this situation?"

I dropped into Britain from Mars; Chris and Natasha Ashton dropped into America from Mars. I'm a British success story from America; they're an American success story from Britain that you can emulate in your own business.

Appendix 2
More Books to Guide Your Own Model and Culture

Here are some titles my team and I recommend to anyone starting out in business.

Built From Scratch: How A Couple of Regular Guys Built The Home Depot from Nothing to $30 Billion, by Bernie Marcus and Arthur Blank with Bob Andelman, Crown Business, 2001

Enchantment: The Art of Changing Hearts, Minds, and Actions, by Guy Kawasaki, Portfolio, 2012

Four Seasons: The Story of a Business Philosophy, by Isadore Sharp, Portfolio, 2012

The Happiness Advantage: The Seven Principles of Positive Psychology That Fuel Success and Performance at Work, by Shawn Achor, Crown Business, 2010

Mavericks At Work: Why the Most Original Minds in Business Win, by William Taylor and Polly LaBarre, Harper, 2008

Reality Check: The Irreverent Guide to Outsmarting, Outmanaging, and Outmarketing Your Competition, by Guy Kawasaki, Portfolio, 2011

Index